CW00969141

The Easy Indian Slow Cooker Cookbook

The Easy Indian Slow Cooker Cookbook

Prep-and-Go Restaurant Favorites
to Make at Home

Hari Ghotra

Foreword by Vivek Singh, author and executive chef
and CEO of The Cinnamon Club

Photography by Hélène Dujardin

ROCKRIDGE
PRESS

Copyright © 2017 by Hari Ghotra

No part of this publication may be reproduced, stored in a retrieval system or transmitted in any form or by any means, electronic, mechanical, photocopying, recording, scanning or otherwise, except as permitted under Sections 107 or 108 of the 1976 United States Copyright Act, without the prior written permission of the Publisher. Requests to the Publisher for permission should be addressed to the Permissions Department, Rockridge Press, 918 Parker St, Suite A-12, Berkeley, CA 94710.

Limit of Liability/Disclaimer of Warranty: The Publisher and the author make no representations or warranties with respect to the accuracy or completeness of the contents of this work and specifically disclaim all warranties, including without limitation warranties of fitness for a particular purpose. No warranty may be created or extended by sales or promotional materials. The advice and strategies contained herein may not be suitable for every situation. This work is sold with the understanding that the publisher is not engaged in rendering medical, legal or other professional advice or services. If professional assistance is required, the services of a competent professional person should be sought. Neither the Publisher nor the author shall be liable for damages arising herefrom. The fact that an individual, organization or website is referred to in this work as a citation and/or potential source of further information does not mean that the author or the Publisher endorses the information the individual, organization or website may provide or recommendations they/it may make. Further, readers should be aware that Internet websites listed in this work may have changed or disappeared between when this work was written and when it is read.

For general information on our other products and services or to obtain technical support, please contact our Customer Care Department within the U.S. at (866) 744-2665, or outside the U.S. at (510) 253-0500.

Rockridge Press publishes its books in a variety of electronic and print formats. Some content that appears in print may not be available in electronic books, and vice versa.

TRADEMARKS: Rockridge Press and the Rockridge Press logo are trademarks or registered trademarks of Callisto Media Inc. and/or its affiliates, in the United States and other countries, and may not be used without written permission. All other trademarks are the property of their respective owners. Rockridge Press is not associated with any product or vendor mentioned in this book.

Photography © 2017 Hélène Dujardin. Food styling by Tami Hardeman, prop styling by Angela Hall. Additional photography: Andrzej Bochenski/Shutterstock.com, page xiv; author photo © 2017 Hari Ghotra.

Illustrations © 2017 Tom Bingham.

ISBN: Print 978-1-62315-969-6
eBook 978-1-62315-970-2

Simply for Mr. Nirmal Singh Ghotra,
my dad, my hero, my legend!

Contents

Five: Dhal (Lentils and Beans) 69

Six: Vegetables 85

Seven: Chicken 105

Eight: Lamb, Pork, and Beef — 127

Nine: Sweets and Desserts — 151

Ten: Chutneys and Staples — 165

Foreword

GROWING UP IN THE EASTERN REGION OF BENGAL, some of my earliest memories were the big social gatherings and celebrations in my hometown. The festivities themselves were quite spectacular, but what I remember most were the fascinating scenes behind the food preparation for the 500 or so expected guests. Because of the massive size of these events, the planners hired professional chefs who worked around the clock to make sure the food was the center of the attraction. It was a special treat for everyone involved, especially for the head matriarch who normally managed the day-to-day cooking.

These guys would start at the crack of dawn, going around the neighborhood in search of bricks to build and cement a makeshift hearth large enough to accommodate the massive pots and servings. For one particular occasion, I vividly recall seeing an enormous side of lamb next to about 45 pounds of rice meant for a gigantic pot of biryani! With the *mise en place* set—vegetables cleaned and prepped, the meat trimmed and seasoned, and the spices mixed together and set aside—the chefs proceeded to create layers of rice, veggies, spices, and lamb.

Then, with all the bricks in place, they scattered bundles of wood and bark at the bottom of the hearth and got two big fires going for the pot of ingredients. Mind you, by this point of the cooking process, it was barely eight in the morning. My childhood self was sure that there must be a mistake, because the party wasn't scheduled to start until eight or nine in the evening. I had to wonder if the dinner event was in fact a lunch event, because no one in their right mind would have a pot of food cooking over a roaring fire for twelve hours!

But what happened next cleared up any confusion. Once the ingredients were brought to a boil, the chefs removed that behemoth pot from the open flames and gingerly placed it on a bed of slow-burning wood at the bottom of the hearth. Then, hot coals were placed on top of the lid to produce just the right amount of heat to keep the pot simmering for the next twelve hours, just like what one would expect from a slow cooker appliance—a life-saving tool for today's busy, multitasking household. And I'm pretty sure those harried chefs felt the same way about their version of slow cooking. With their hands free of the biryani, they used the remaining time to complete the rest of the menu for that night's sumptuous dinner.

Not too long after sunset, crowds of people started to file inside the marquee. It was time to bring out the pièce de résistance. As the chefs and servers removed the coals and then the lid, ribbons of steam escaped the pot, sending out a heavenly aroma. The scent, becoming exceedingly stronger as guests filled their individual plates, was so intoxicating that I'm willing to bet that people who forgot about the event or who were taking their time to arrive were instantly reminded and compelled to rush to the festivities the moment they got a whiff of that perfectly cooked lamb biryani.

And the inviting and mesmerizing scent was just a precursor. Tasting the different layers of fluffy rice, tender flaky meat, and the burst of spices took the sensory experience to another level. By allowing the ingredients the time to reach a beautiful balance of soft textures and bold flavors, the chefs achieved what they set out to do. That biryani still stands out as one of those life-changing food experiences—not only because of how it tasted, but also because of the effort, the love, and the time that went into producing a special meal that brought people together.

Throughout my decades-long career as a chef, teacher, book author, curator of recipes, and advocate for Indian food, the lessons from that biryani still hold true: the best food is made when a lot of love is put into the preparation and cooking of a dish or meal—which almost always means cooking slow and low—and that these loving methods are the basis of traditional Indian cooking. But in this digital and tech era of apps, smartphones, and global communication and markets, slow and low is swapped for fast and instant. Especially when it comes to Indian cooking, many people don't want to bother with the spices, the prep, and the time needed to make homemade biryani when they can get it quickly from a restaurant. And with more and more people relying on takeout menus and associating Indian cuisine with the fast food version, experiences like the biryani from my childhood are rare at best and mainly seen as an inconvenience. As a people and culture with advanced tools and resources at our fingertips, we often find ourselves trading in these lasting impressions for fleeting moments of instant gratification and convenience. How do we find a balance that allows us to experience the joys of a thoughtful, wholesome meal while meeting the demands of modern-day life?

In her book *The Easy Indian Slow Cooker Cookbook*, Hari Ghotra takes on this challenge with steady persistence, genuine enthusiasm, and with the help of her slow cooker. Using essential cooking skills and techniques from her training as a chef in Michelin-starred restaurants and focusing on simple, quality ingredients that her legions of blog readers know her for, Hari has developed the best Indian recipes specially adapted for this must-have appliance. With her insight and guidance, we discover the endless possibilities and benefits when you combine the traditions of Indian cuisine with the modern magic of the slow cooker. Budget cuts of meat that would otherwise be impossible to cook on a regular stove fall off of the bone in a vindaloo or tikka masala, delivering an unforgettably hearty meal at an affordable price. Legumes and beans are cooked to creamy consistencies, eliminating the need for added dairy, and natural oils are extracted when Indian spices are set on a low simmer, reducing fat while maintaining maximum flavor.

While thoughts of simpler times and of makeshift hearths amidst the current hustle and bustle remind us that some things are meant to stay in the past, Hari proves that the true essence of Indian cooking, or any kind of good home cooking, is never lost when you put the effort, love, and care into your everyday meals—fast or slow.

–Vivek Singh, author and executive chef
and CEO of The Cinnamon Club

Introduction

Indian Slow Food
Is the Best Kind of Fast Food

THE REALITIES OF slow cooking and fast food seem worlds apart, especially when it comes to Indian food. Indian fast food is what you get delivered when you crave those pungent spices and some chile heat to warm the soul. The assumption is that Indian food is difficult to prepare, is time-consuming, is expensive (because of all those spices), and takes a lot of effort to understand the ingredients and different cooking techniques. With the busy lives we lead, cooking Indian food from scratch seems like another headache we just don't need. And to stand over a pot, stirring and following complicated recipes for hours, just pushes most of us to reach for that takeout menu.

Unfortunately, when it comes to takeout, you have no control over what is in the food. There are no guidelines on fat, salt, and sugar contents, the quality of the ingredients is a mystery, and over the long term, it's an expensive way to get your curry fix. In my opinion, a lot of takeout dishes don't represent the best of Indian food, because they all tend to taste the same. It's difficult to achieve authentic flavors if the right cooking methods aren't used, and it doesn't help when everything is finished with additional (and unnecessary) cream or butter. Although occasionally it's fine to indulge, this option is hurting both our wallets and our waistlines, and it doesn't even really represent what great Indian food is all about! If cooked slowly, urid beans (black

gram) naturally become creamy, and meat will soak up the aromatics from the spices and take on an intense flavor while having a melt-in-your-mouth consistency.

I love the fact that the desire to taste Indian food is growing—and I am here to tell you that takeout isn't the only option. I have grown up eating great Indian food all my life. It was always cooked fresh by my mum with beautifully vibrant ingredients, quickly and easily. From simple lentil dhals to exotic biryanis, everything was made with love, very little fat, and complex layers of flavors. I picked up hints and tips about how to use spices effectively and how to get the most out of both vegetables and meat to produce light, fragrant meals. Many of the dishes I grew up with and now cook for my family are a far cry from the food found on restaurant and takeout menus. Home-cooked dishes are more basic and are centered around providing a rounded meal that's healthy and good for the mind and soul.

I grew up in England with parents who came to the United Kingdom from India in the 1960s. They brought with them the desire to improve their lives but also an imperative to hold on to everything that was special about the Indian way of life. Family, culture, and religion were top priorities, and food was on the top of the list as well.

My mum often speaks to me about how she used to cook in India, using outdoor stoves, and how they would plan the next day's meal ahead of time so they could make the most of the ingredients and even of the flames in the stove. Lentils would be cooked over the dying embers of the fire and left overnight to simmer away gently, resulting in the creamiest dhal without using any pats of butter. Meat would be carefully marinated with delicate spices and layered with rice into a *handi* (a deep, wide-mouthed clay pot). The vessel was sealed shut with dough and left for hours to cook on a bed of hot coals (a technique called *dhum*), and it would prepare so slowly that the flavors would have ample time to soak through the grains of puffed-up rice. The ceremonious opening of the handi the next day would be a family event. The dough would be cracked open and the aromatic fragrances of the spices would fill the air. There's an old Indian saying that there's no need to invite people to come over to eat biryani, because as soon as the handi is opened, the heavenly aromas float through the air to friends and family, and they all eventually arrive anyway.

Throughout my childhood, my parents would try to replicate these outdoor cooking techniques in an attempt to recapture the flavors of their childhoods and remind themselves of home. As an Indian chef, I've learned about traditional techniques, according to which meat and vegetables are cooked low and slow, to produce some of the beautiful dishes we know and love—from creamy black dhal to tandoori chicken to dhum biryani. And the slow cooker is the ideal tool to create these authentic flavors, because in many ways it uses the same principles of low and slow in a sealed pot, producing flavorful food that is just as vibrant and healthy as what my mum made for me when I was a child.

The slow-cooker recipes in this book are easy and perfect for home cooks and restaurant goers alike, delivering some of the most popular and frequently ordered Indian food straight to your home dining table—and all without having to reach for a takeout menu.

Chapter One

Slow Cooking Indian Food

India (or Hindustan, as Indian people actually call it) is a vast, vibrant, and culturally rich country. The people are friendly and hospitable, with colorful personalities. The languages and dialects are loud and confusing, but the smiles are warm and welcoming. The country itself is a huge landmass with probably one of the most diverse terrains. From the vast majestic Himalayan mountain range of the Northern frontier to the tropical coastal beaches of the South, from dense forest areas to the watershed regions on the Bangladesh boarder, India has deserts, plains, landlocked regions, and mighty rivers.

Over the centuries, these cultural and geographical landscapes have influenced Indian cuisine. Much of the food that is consumed in India is produced locally, so the cooking style is representative of each location. From the communal village tandoors of the Punjab to the hand-ground spice pastes of the South, every region has a style and a selection of ingredients and spices used in everyday cooking.

History

India is a country shaped by its long history of invasions and colonization, having been ruled in areas by the French, the Portuguese, the British, and many other nations. To identify these colonial influences, one need only study India's cuisine. As outside cultures influenced India and its people, so did new ingredients and cooking techniques. The result was new hybrid dishes that we now instantly identify as popular staples in Indian cuisine and that can be found in almost every Indian restaurant across major cities.

Vindaloo and xacuti are dishes with Portuguese roots. Along with potatoes and tomatoes, the Portuguese introduced chiles to India. And today India is the number one producer of the cayenne pepper.

Religion and Culture

India is one of the most culturally diverse countries in the world, and its different religions strongly influence what people eat and enjoy. Cuisines are strictly classified as vegetarian or nonvegetarian, emphasizing the need for dietary restrictions and specifications based on a person's religious beliefs and way of life. Hindus and Sikhs, for example, are forbidden by their religion to consume beef, Muslims do not eat pork, many Buddhists are vegetarian or vegan, and so on. Poverty is also a huge problem in India, and simple lentils and dhals provide much-needed protein and other nutrients for many people.

The Regions

The climate significantly changes across the country, from alpine through to equatorial, influencing the characteristics and availability of local ingredients and produce. The South, with scorching hot summers and drenching monsoon seasons, is India's spice garden, where peppercorns, cardamom, and cloves can be found in abundance. The cold, harsh winters in the North make for amazingly fertile soil, resulting in vast farming areas like the Punjab, the land of milk and honey. The dry heat of the West gives rise to such foods as gram (chickpea) flour, which is regularly used in spiced Indian cakes and snacks. The wet Eastern side of India means fish, fish, and more fish. Each area has local produce specific to that region, and this varies across the country.

The South

This region is known as the garden of India, teeming with fragrant, locally grown spices, such as cardamom, cinnamon, and cassia. The coastal regions offer an abundance of coconut, tamarind, and seafood. The style of cooking is all about curry leaves and mustard seeds, with an emphasis on ginger. Hot, pungent spice pastes are created from chiles, spices, coconut, and tamarind, and coconut oil is used for cooking. Using these strong spice pastes, the sauces are then finished with coconut milk to give a balanced sauce that is perfectly sweet, hot, and creamy.

The North

The Punjab is a state in North India known for its fertile lands; the economy here is rich in farming and agriculture. Wheat is a staple, so breads such as roti, naan, and flatbreads are served with just about every meal. Onion, ginger, garlic, green chiles, and tomatoes form the base of most dishes, so the masala (a signature spice blend) is rich and flavorful. Garam masala is the iconic spice blend of the North, and is all about using spices to create warmth.

The West

With its arid climate, cooking in the West uses strong spices, which are ideal for pickling and fermenting. Jaggery (unrefined cane sugar) or some other form of sweetness is injected into savory dishes to create sweet-and-sour flavors in the state of Gujarat. Rajasthan is about red meat and simple cooking methods using asafetida, fennel, and ginger powders.

The East

In the East, each meal includes some type of freshwater fish. A strong Mongolian–Chinese influence is also seen with momos (a kind of dumpling), rice dishes, and the use of panch phoran, which is a whole-spice blend from the area.

From village to village and from state to state, the people of each area have their own way of cooking. To catalog it all would be impossible—there is simply so much going on across India's food landscape. This is probably why the food of this beautiful, vibrant country has been distilled into what is now available on Indian restaurant

Regional Food of India

Northern Region

Climate: Hot summers and cold winters

Regions: Punjab, Jammu and Kashmir, Uttar Pardesh and Hiryana.

Culinary influence: Mughal

Typical dish and food: Rogan Josh

Punjab
- Food is heavily influenced by agricultural landscape rich in vegetables, grains, legumes, and sugar canes.
- Also known for producing dairy (yogurt, lassi, makan, ghee)
- Foods tend to be mild. Onion, garlic, and the regional main spice garam masala are used to create a thick and rich sauce with layers of flavor.

Kashmir
- Mogul influences and rich diet of red meat, yogurt, and rice.
- Known for huge banquets and elaborate dishes such as biryani.

Eastern Region

Climate: Wet

Regions: Bengal

Culinary influences: Chinese and Mongolian

Regional overview: Lots of green plants and vegetables, fruit, and grains, namely rice. Coastal regions promote a rich diet of fish and seafood. Pork is popular inland. These regions are also known for their sweets and desserts.

Typical dishes and food: momos (steam-filled wontons), fish curry

Bengal
- Meals start with a bitter dish, then lentils, fish, vegetables, and meat are served separately.
- Panch phoran is the spice blend of choice.

Western Region

Climate: Hot and dry

Regions: Rajasthan, Gujarat, Goa

Culinary influence: Hindu

Regional overview: Food is spicy and with few vegetables available, pickling is common. Staples include corn, lentils, gram flour, and yogurt.

Typical dishes and food: vindaloo, fish curry, patia sauce

Rajasthan
- Rich diet of red meat
- Known for biryanis, dried fruits and nuts
- Range of spicy to sour dishes

Gujarat
- Jaggery is used as a sweetener
- Small dishes served in a thali

Goa
- Coastal region rich in coconut, peanuts, rice, and fish and seafood
- Huge Portuguese influence, namely with vinegar used in sauces

Southern Region

Climate: Lots of rain. Hot and humid.

Regions: Hydrabad, Karela

Regional overview: Spice garden of India; abundant in tamarind, asafetida, mustard seeds, peppercorns, chilies, and coconut. The main staple is rice and used in different recipes.

Typical dishes: idlis, dosa, rasam, sambar, papadums

Hydrabad
- Known for raw meat biryanis, dried fruits, nuts, and saffron
- Flavors range from spicy to sour

Karela
- Coastal region abundant in fish and seafood, fruit, vegetables, and coconut.
- Cuisine is mainly vegetarian with hot and fiery dishes made through the use of spice pastes

menus. Versions of key dishes have been created in generic ways, to make sense of the complex and varied cuisine for a public that is unfamiliar with it. The early restaurateurs who came from the Punjab and Bangladesh had to establish a way of communicating to their customers what those dishes were, so an arbitrary scale came into being where a korma is mild, moving up the ranks to a madras, and right through to a phaal (which is burning-chile hot). In reality, this isn't how Indian people eat. You cook to suit your palate, and spice the dish accordingly.

With all this being said, I think it's important to recognize that restaurants and takeout places have actually done a lot over the years in spreading acceptance of Indian food and encouraging people to try new, unfamiliar flavors.

Favorite Indian Dishes

Wherever you go in the world, Indian restaurants have the old favorites on the menu. When I worked at a top London restaurant, the orders for tikka masala still came through to the kitchen even though the item wasn't on the menu—and the reason for that was simple, as most people's experience of Indian food begins with trying these restaurant favorites. Whether they are authentic or not, they are loved across the world, and I think it's something we should embrace and be proud of.

Tandoori

Tandoori is more about the style of cooking rather than the dish itself. A tandoor is a traditional bell-shaped clay oven that is charcoal- or wood-fired. Made from a special clay, it can be heated to very high temperatures without crumbling. The oven retains the heat for long periods of time and produces very succulent meat that is moist and has a wonderful smoky flavor. A classic tandoori marinade is a two-stage process: first, lemon, ginger, garlic, green chile, and salt are used to start the tenderizing process, then a yogurt-based second marinade helps infuse the spices into the meat and protect it while cooking at the high temperature of the tandoor. The yogurt is first hung in a muslin cloth to drain out excess liquid. It's then mixed with garam masala, warming ground cumin seed, Kashmiri chili powder (for the vibrant red color), oil (I use mustard oil to add smokiness), and dried fenugreek leaves.

Vindaloo

I love talking about vindaloo. It's a dish with loads of history that has been modified to suit our needs. In 1980s England it was the dish of choice after a beer on a Friday night, and was all about the heat level. In fact, vindaloo is a uniquely flavored dish from the state of Goa; the dish has Portuguese roots and is a great example of India's culinary history. The Portuguese arrived in India in the 1500s, bringing with them chiles from Latin America, along with other European culinary influences, such as wine. Many Goans converted to Christianity, so eating pork was no longer forbidden, and the meat has since become an inherent part of Goan food.

This original Portuguese stew dish, *carne de vinha d'ahlos*, was pork marinated in red wine and garlic. The vin, or wine, was eventually switched out for vinegar and Kashmiri chiles. In Goa, this dish is known as *vindahlo*—a combination of *vin* (vinegar) and *ahlo*, the Portuguese word for garlic. The result is a wonderfully spiced pork-and-garlic stew with a tangy sourness that can be as hot or as mild as you like.

Saag

Saag is a generic word for mixed greens. Though you can use kale, mustard greens, or collard greens, spinach is most commonly used. Saag is a delicacy from the Punjab region, where it's made with the distinctly flavored mustard greens. Saag, as a puréed spinach dish, is typically eaten at Vaisakhi, the Punjabi harvest festival that marks the birth of Sikhism. In restaurants, saag comes in a number of dishes, with either paneer or potatoes (saag aloo). At home, we tend to eat saag as a puréed spinach dish with roti (a cornstarch flatbread).

I can remember this dish taking my mum the whole day to prepare, from cooking the greens down to blending them by hand, and then recooking. But with the invention of slow cookers and electric blenders, this is the perfect dish to cook low and slow—no need to add any cream, and butter is optional!

Biryani

Steeped in history, biryanis are thought to have originated during the years of the Mughal Raj (or empire, which spanned the 1500s through to the mid-1800s). Marking a symbol of wealth, a decadent biryani would have been served at huge celebratory feasts for the courtiers. The dish was brought together using the most expensive whole spices, from cloves to saffron, with a variety of different meats to make it look even more spectacular (and expensive!). The biryani would be brought to the table on huge platters, topped off with cooked meats stuffed into other meats—just imagine a whole goat stuffed with mutton stuffed with quail.

There are two types of biryanis: the one from Hyderabad uses raw marinated mutton cooked in the dhum style, and the Lucknow biryani uses meat prepared in a cooked masala. Made either way, it's all about a one-pot rice-and-meat dish that is so fragrant that each mouthful pops with new flavor and delight.

Butter Chicken

In Punjabi, the term for butter chicken is *murgh makhani*, and you'll find it listed that way on most restaurant menus. It's a wonderfully rich dish that has a vivid orange-red sauce because it's cooked with fresh, ripe tomatoes, a few key spices, and a little butter. Translated, the word *makhani* literally means "with butter." Its roots are firmly planted in the Punjab region, where it's thought to have been developed by chefs from the Moti Mahal Hotel restaurant in Delhi.

It's mildly spiced and has a beautiful balance of flavors, from the earthiness of the dried fenugreek leaves to the sweetness of honey. And for a little restaurant decadence, you can finish the plate with a dash of cream. A perfect family dish!

Tikka Masala

The universally favorite restaurant dish, tikka masala is most people's first experience with Indian food. Although it's not a dish I grew up eating, I can see why we all love it. It's thought to have originated in the United Kingdom, with a restaurateur, as a way for him to reuse the chicken cooked in the tandoor oven. In restaurants, the chicken is marinated and cooked on skewers in a tandoor, so it's succulent and juicy. The masala is flavored with a cashew paste to give it a nutty texture and a creamy finish. Some restaurants use peppers and red onions, and finish the dish with a little cream, creating a delicious curry.

Dhal Makhani

This is a classic North Indian dish traditionally cooked low and slow, overnight on a flame, which gives it its natural buttery texture. It's considered a poor man's dish, but is so rich in protein that it's a wonderful alternative to meat. The black lentils are usually presoaked overnight, and once softened they are cooked simply with onions, tomatoes, ginger, garlic, and a chile or two. This is pure soul food, and in a slow cooker there is no need to presoak—just leave it to do its thing.

Chana Masala

Chickpeas (chana) are a real staple in the Indian home. We use them in so many different ways, from curries to spicy snacks to grinding them into a flour for making a great batter. Chana masala is essentially a chickpea curry dish that has several iterations. Sometimes I cook the chickpeas in tea to achieve a deep earthiness; sometimes I make them dry with chaat masala, red onions, and sliced green chiles for a satisfying kick of spice; and other times just a simple tomato masala will do, served with fried poori (a popular flatbread).

Indian Food Cooked Slowly

A slow cooker is an electric countertop cooking pot that keeps food simmering at a low temperature over a long period of time. It essentially enables you to cook dishes unattended, allowing you to make more of your day, and giving you the luxury to come home to a healthy home-cooked meal after a long day at work.

I have used a slow cooker for many years, because providing my family with homemade food is important to me. Working long hours as a chef and as a food writer, my days are busy and irregular. My slow cooker allows me to feed my family even when I'm gone all day.

Many Indian dishes are all about low-and-slow cooking methods, allowing the flavors of the spices to infuse the dish to produce rich, flavorful sauces that are as aromatic as they are delicious. The slow cooker saves time, allowing you to cook healthy dishes using fresh ingredients for great everyday cooking. From vegetable dishes, to legumes and dhals, to tender meat-based curries—all these are perfect for the slow cooker, as the device effectively replicates classic Indian cooking techniques, and requires little preparation.

Traditionally a masala, the base of curries, is created by tempering the spices—briefly toasting them in oil to get a base flavor—and sautéing onions to a rich and dark golden brown, then adding aromatic ingredients such as garlic, ginger, and chiles. The meat or main ingredients are then added and left to cook low and slow. For this book, I have tweaked traditional recipes to create minimal preparation time, so the ingredients can be tossed into the slow cooker and left alone. Some dishes can even be left to cook overnight.

That said, certain dishes do require precooking and some prep work, but this should take no longer than 15 minutes. If you do have the time, you can brown your ingredients first (typically, the onions, garlic, ginger, and meat), for that additional flavor. But if you lack the time, throw it all in the pot and let it do its thing—your meal will still be delicious.

The recipes in chapters 3 through 9 were developed specifically for your slow cooker. But there are also a number of accompanying dishes that I felt needed to be included to complete this Indian cookbook that are not suited for the slow cooker.

Using Your Slow Cooker: Dos and Don'ts

Do

- Lightly season your dish at the beginning of cooking. The slow cooking will concentrate the sauce, so it's best to adjust the seasonings later to prevent your dish from being too salty or spicy. You can also add delicate vegetables and ingredients toward the end of the cooking time, so they don't overcook.
- Spray the inside of your slow cooker with a nonstick cooking spray, which makes cleaning it easier.
- Choose your meat carefully, as you don't want it all to disintegrate. The following cuts are great.

  Beef: go for shin, stewing steak, skirt, brisket, or topside
  Chicken: meat on the bone is best, either thighs or drumsticks.
  Pork: shoulder and neck work really well
  Lamb: shoulder, rump, neck, and leg joints

- Trim the excess fat. Although you are not adding any extra oil to the dish, with slow cooking, the fat from the meat will remain in the dish and can make it greasy.
- Slow cookers are meant to cook unattended, so resist constantly checking the dish. Each time you remove the lid, the pot releases heat, which means the cooking time has to be increased.
- Read the full recipe all the way through so you understand all the steps before getting started.

Don't

- Don't add too much liquid—you only need enough to just cover the ingredients. And the lid is tight fitting, so the liquid won't evaporate.
- Don't cook frozen food in your slow cooker. It takes too long for the food to reach a safe temperature, so thaw meat completely before cooking it. You can add a small amount of frozen vegetables toward the end of cooking; this won't affect the cooking time.
- Do not heat leftovers in a slow cooker because they will not reach the temperatures required to be safe for consumption.
- Don't over- or under-fill your cooker. It can be dangerous and will negatively affect the way the food cooks.
- Don't clean your slow cooker with abrasive cleaners or scrubbers, as this damages the cooking insert.

Know Your Slow Cooker

There are multitudes of slow cookers on the market, from the very basic to the new fancy ones with exotic functions. They come in various shapes, from round to oval, and different sizes.

SHAPE

Most slow cookers are either round or oval, and both cook just as well. When choosing one for your needs, consider the types of dishes you will be cooking. For example, if you will be cooking whole joints, ribs, brisket, or entire chickens, then an oval dish may be a better choice. But if you are more likely to be cooking curries and stews, shape doesn't really matter—you just need a cooker that will fit in your kitchen cabinet or neatly sit on your countertop.

SIZE

From tiny cookers to huge-capacity cookers, you need to consider what will best suit your family. The key point to remember with slow cookers is that the pot needs to be at least half-full to get good results. For a small household, if you are not keen on leftovers (and you are happy to scale down recipes), a 3- or 4-quart (3- to 4-liter) cooker will be perfect.

An average-size cooker is about 6 quarts, and is probably the one I would recommend you start with. If however you cook for bigger groups or like to double up recipes, a bigger pot is more suitable. Look for an 8-quart slow cooker.

To cook the recipes in this book, I have used a 4-quart KitchenAid Multi-Cooker, which is perfect for cooking about six portions. This multi-cooker is fantastic because it gives you the option for sautéing, a perfect feature for quickly tempering spices and browning onions. It also has a yogurt function and a rice-cooker function, which makes this a great option if you are looking to invest in a slow cooker, especially for making Indian food.

Recipes can also easily be halved and prepared in a smaller 3-quart cooker. Just make sure that you reduce the amount of liquid by half. In terms of the spices and other ingredients, you may want to reduce them slightly, but not by half. If you are cooking for a larger group (or you want some leftovers), recipes can simply be bulked out and doubled.

IMPORTANT FUNCTIONS

Many of the newer cookers let you cook in different ways in the pot itself. If you have a cooker with these additional functions, then some of the cooking processes in the recipes here can be done directly in the pot, making cooking them even easier. If you have an older-style slow cooker, please don't worry—these recipes can still be made in them. You'll just have to do a little bit of cooking on the stovetop before transferring to the slow cooker.

Timer If you are always going to be around when you use your slow cooker, then you don't need to worry about a timer. But having this function gives you flexibility, as the pot will turn itself off once the cooking has finished, preventing overcooking.

Warming function I think an automatic warming function is essential. Once the cooking is complete, the cooker will automatically switch to "warm" mode. This feature keeps your food at a lower temperature, so that it stays warm but doesn't overcook the dish. It's also a great way for food to stay warm while you are hosting guests.

Sear function Searing meat adds color, which in turn adds flavor, so this is a great function to have on your slow cooker. Some slow cookers have an insert that can be removed and placed directly onto the stovetop to sear meat. With other cookers you can sear directly in the insert before the slow cooking starts. Either way, it means there is less washing up to do—always a good thing.

COOKING TIMES

Each of my recipes will state cooking times on both a high and a low setting, so you can cook the dishes according to your schedule. I personally prefer to cook on the low setting because I find that the results are tastier. The low setting allows the flavors of the spices to infuse into the dish and makes meat much more tender and giving it a delicious melt-in-your-mouth feel. Sauces also thicken better and the overall result is smoother. That said, I totally understand that we all have routines that govern how our days unfold, so do what suits you and your family.

GENERAL GUIDELINES ON COOKING TIMES

Stovetop cooking time	Slow cooker on high	Slow cooker on low
15 to 30 minutes	1 to 2 hours	4 to 6 hours
30 minutes to 1 hour	2 to 3 hours	5 to 7 hours
1 to 2 hours	3 to 4 hours	6 to 8 hours
2 to 4 hours	4 to 6 hours	8 to 12 hours

Chapter Two

The Indian Kitchen

The kitchen was the hub of our home when I was young, even though it was tiny. Mum was forever busy doing something in there—grinding spices, chopping vegetables—and the stove was always on and there was always a pot that needed stirring.

I can remember standing on a plastic stool peering into a huge stainless-steel pan with a wooden spoon in hand, feeling very grown up as I had been given the task of stirring the onions while my mum got the concoction of colorful spices ready. One by one she added them to the pan, telling me what each one was—tomatoes, haldi (turmeric), jeera (cumin), mirch (pepper), a little more haldi. Everything was done by eye until it looked right—not a teaspoon in sight.

I was always amazed at how the onions changed to a paste, and then I would get excited as I knew mum would dollop some of the masala on a slice of bread just for me! I was introduced to spices and chiles pretty early on, and even though I would munch away and end up coughing and spluttering as the chile caught the back of my throat, I couldn't have been happier!

Classic Cooking Techniques

There are a number of classic Indian cooking techniques that are used in authentic Indian stovetop cooking. They all play a part in infusing a dish with flavor and aromatics, and are used differently for different dishes. These include:

Tharka

Tharka involves tempering whole spices in hot oil or ghee to intensify their natural flavors, creating a fragrant oil that is used either at the beginning of the cooking process as the base flavor of the dish, or in some cases (such as with some dhals) as the final garnish.

Bhuna

To sauté and brown (usually onions) over a low-and-slow heat at the start of the cooking process, creating real depth and intensity for the base masala, letting the onions just melt away into the sauce. You can also bhun meat dishes at the end of the cooking time over a high heat to reduce the sauce and intensify the flavor of the masala, so it clings to the meat.

Dhuna

This is a more unusual process—using burning charcoal in a closed pot to infuse a smoky flavor. I use this with some chutneys to impart them with earthiness and a smoked quality. I make a foil tray and set it inside the pan, place the hot coals on the foil tray, add some whole spices and a tablespoon of ghee so it begins to smoke. Then I put the lid on the pan and leave the smoke to infuse into the dish for 10 to 15 minutes.

Dhum

Essentially steaming or simmering on very low heat over a long cooking period in a vessel that is sealed closed using dough. The results of this method are very close to those achieved by a slow cooker. This is the traditional way of cooking a biryani, where rice and spiced meat are layered, allowing the fragrance of the spices to infuse the rice.

These methods are made for stovetop cooking, but for this book I have tried to simplify the authentic techniques to help you cook great-tasting and healthy Indian food from scratch at home in the simplest way possible. The recipes are designed to be achievable as written. I have tried to keep the use of other equipment to a minimum, unless an item is essential for a specific recipe.

I will also include a number of hints and tips so you are able to convert stovetop-cooking techniques to the slow cooker.

The Indian Pantry

Like with any specialty style of cooking, you'll need to stock up on a few essentials, and from my years of teaching people about Indian food I understand that spices can be a bit of a showstopper for some. Selecting the right ones can feel a little intimidating. Where do you go for these ingredients? How do you know you are getting value for your money? How do you know they will be any good?

First, I think it's important to understand that you don't need to spend a fortune. Don't go out and immediately buy every single spice and ingredient in this book. Make one recipe at a time and build your spice collection as you progress. I usually recommend buying your spices whole and grinding them in a mortar and pestle, or in a spice grinder, as needed. Whole spices (if stored correctly) will hold their natural oils for longer than when they are ground, and therefore whole spices are more pungent when cooking with them—plus they will keep for longer.

Second, I have tried to ensure that the ingredients called for can be used across a number of different recipes, so there are no one-use purchases required.

If you have an Indian grocery store near you, this is your first port of call. If not, most supermarkets these days are well stocked with Indian ingredients. The other option is to look online, where you will be able to get everything you need. Check out the Resources section of this book, where I list some great online stores for Indian spices and supplies.

Once you have a well-stocked Indian pantry, you will find that you use the ingredients time and time again—in other types of dishes, too—so you won't be wasting your money. Many of the lentils, beans, flours, and nuts are dried, so they will keep for a long time. Fresh ingredients such as chiles, coriander (called "cilantro" in North America), ginger, and garlic are best bought when you require them. If you don't use them all, freeze them and use again when needed.

Indian Spices

Indian food is all about mastering combinations of spices and adding layers of flavor that leave you yearning for more. Most people tend to be too heavy-handed when it comes to spices, adding the same spices to every curry dish they make, so everything tastes identical regardless of the other ingredients. But authentic Indian food is not about creating a dish so spicy you can't taste the flavors of the ingredients, and it's not about making dishes that all taste the same.

Spices can be categorized into groups, depending on how they should be used during the cooking process.

Whole spices are generally tempered, which means they are heated in hot oil at the beginning of the cooking process to release their natural oils. These include cassia bark, green cardamom, cloves, cumin seeds, mustard seeds, and bay leaves.

Taste and color spices are added to the pan one at a time, usually midway through the recipe. They are typically in powder form and should be added to a liquid base—for example, after the tomatoes have gone in. Chili, coriander, and turmeric powders are all taste and color spices.

Flavor spices are more delicate, such as cardamom and mace powders, and are used to enhance flavor profiles. They tend to be added toward the end of the cooking process. Delicate herbs, like fresh coriander and fenugreek, will also go in at the end.

Prep: It's Quicker Than You Think

I know you may look at some of the recipes and think, "That's a lot of spices—and it's going to be a lot of work!" Don't be intimidated by a long ingredients list; most of it is just the spices, and they are the easiest bit to get ready and require the least amount of preparation (sometimes none at all). The most difficult part is getting your spices together—but once you have a stock of the essential spices, the hard part is done. All you do then is just pull out a few jars and measuring spoons.

Before I start cooking, I always get the spices ready first by measuring them all out onto a plate. This way, I am practically halfway through the recipe before I even start. I also like to keep my mortar and pestle accessible, as I find that it makes things easier and I am more inclined to use it.

With the recipes in this book, I have tried to stick to this process of adding spices at different times and in different forms. The whole spices are tempered in a frying pan or directly in your slow cooker (if yours has a sear function). This will heat the oil and spices effectively at the start of the dish to create the base flavors. The taste and color spices are then added with the main ingredients. And the final flavor spices are added just before serving the dish.

I have listed essential and nonessential spices, so you can decide which ones you want to shop for first.

Must-Have Spices

Being the essentials for basic Indian dishes, I think these spices are the ones you will need most often. And you will probably find you have a few of them already. For things like cumin and coriander, I usually buy my spices whole and grind them as needed. But if you don't have time to do this, then by all means buy them preground.

Bay leaves (tej patha) Also called laurel, these long, rounded green leaves are generally sold whole and dried. Bay has an herbal and slightly floral fragrance, similar to oregano, which is more prominent than the taste. The leaves enrichen dishes with their unique aroma, which is soft and gives a depth to sauces.

Black peppercorns (kali mirch) These small, round black seeds with a spicy heat are already in every kitchen. Always store in an airtight container and grind them when needed.

Coriander seeds (thania) These small creamy-brown seeds are round, with a gentle citrus flavor and nutty texture. They are warming and fragrant when crushed, but should be stored whole. They're known to help reduce cholesterol, and boiled coriander water can be used as a remedy for colds.

Cumin seeds (jeera) Used whole or ground, these brown crescent-shaped seeds give a warm and pungent flavor, bringing out the natural sweetness of a dish. When used whole they are roasted, which intensifies their flavor. They're high in iron and also help relieve indigestion by stimulating pancreatic enzymes.

Fenugreek (kasoori methi) This is a must-have for Punjabi dishes. This herb comes from the Kasoor region and has a characteristically strong, musky, curry aroma, with a slightly bitter taste. This herb works beautifully when flavoring lamb and dhals, or dishes with a rich, deep sauce. The dried leaves are used for flavoring and the fresh young leaves are used as greens, similar to the way you'd use spinach. Fenugreek seeds, whole or ground, are much more pungent, so it's not a good idea to substitute

Fenugreek

Bay Leaves

Red Chili Powder ▶

Mustard Seeds

Black Peppercorns ▶

Garam Masala

Tumeric

Cumin Seeds

Coriander Seeds

Tame the Heat

There is a misconception that Indian food has to be hot. Yes, we do like our chiles, but Indian cuisine isn't about throwing in lots of chiles to mindlessly kick up the heat. It's about the process of adding spices to get a beautiful layering of flavor. I always suggest that you cook Indian food to suit your palate. There are no rules about how many chiles you "have to" add to a dish. If you prefer foods mild, reduce the chiles, or omit them completely—if you want a more fiery dish, dial the number up. I prefer to use fresh green chiles during the cooking process, which give heat and freshness. Chili powder can be added later to crank up the heat. If you find that your dish is too hot, coconut milk is a good way to add a little sweetness and balance out the spice.

the seeds for the leaves in a recipe. The leaves can be found in most Indian grocery stores, and are widely available dried online.

Garam masala Garam means "warm" and masala is simply a spice blend. Probably one of the most important ingredients of Northern Indian food, the aromatic blend of spices is usually added at the end of the cooking process to intensify and refresh the dish's flavors and fragrances. A typical garam masala includes cumin, black pepper, coriander seeds, cassia bark, carom seeds, black cardamom, cloves, green cardamom, and bay leaves. You can buy premixed garam masala from Indian grocery stores, but if you have time and the desire, I urge you to make your own. You can find my recipe on page 23.

Mustard seeds (sarson) These round seeds may be black, brown, or white. The brown ones are usually used in Indian cooking. When heated, they release a unique flavor—bitter and very pungent. High in magnesium, mustard seeds are known to help lower blood pressure and are a digestive stimulant. Mustard leaves are traditionally used to make saag, the Punjabi dish of puréed greens. Mustard oil, which is very warming, has wide applications—from massaging to cooking.

Red chili powder (lal mirch) Red spicy chili powder is made by grinding dried chiles. My chili powder of choice is Kashmiri chili powder, which is mild in flavor but vivid red in color, imparting vibrancy and smokiness to dishes. Dried bird's-eye chiles significantly raise a dish's hotness profile.

Turmeric (haldi) A member of the ginger family, fresh turmeric looks remarkably like fresh ginger root, only has orange flesh. It is boiled, dried, and ground to make a bright-orange powder. The powder has a chalky texture and a musky, woody aroma that leaves a slight bitter undertone. Regarded as a super spice, turmeric offers many health benefits, including anti-inflammatory and antiseptic properties (both when consumed or when applied externally). It can be used as a paste to treat wounds as well as being a natural decongestant.

Nonessential Spices

These are the spices you might consider for specific dishes, so they are more likely to be one-off buys. But once you become more comfortable cooking Indian food, you'll also want these available in your pantry. Although I do use many of these spices in the recipes here, I don't want you to feel that you have to purchase them right away. If you are just getting started, for now you can do without these items.

Asafetida (hing) This is a powdered resin from a fennel-like plant indigenous to Iran. It has a bitter, acrid flavor, and it stinks a bit. Once tempered, however, it gives a wonderful aroma with a flavor profile similar to onion and garlic. It should only be used in tiny amounts, as hing is very pungent. It's treated as a whole spice and is added to hot oil at the start of the cooking process. Used in lentil and vegetable dishes, hing will give dishes the pungency of onions, even when onions are not actually in the recipe. It's used a lot in Kashmiri, Maharashtrian, and South Indian cooking. Health benefits include antiflatulence properties, as hing is known to be excellent at soothing digestive issues.

Black cardamom (kali elaichi) These large black pods have a deep, earthy, and almost meaty flavor. The pods are dried over flames, giving them a distinct smokiness. They are not eaten, just cracked, and used to infuse flavor into meat and rice dishes. You only need to use one or two pods in any dish.

Carom seeds (ajwain) These tiny oval seeds are very aromatic. When roasted, they release a complex, pungent scent similar to thyme but with a much more warming, dominant flavor. Use them sparingly, as the flavor is strong. They're used in fish and bread dishes, and are known to alleviate stomachaches and to ease indigestion.

Cassia bark (dalchini) This dark-brown outer tree bark is solid, and is thicker and darker than stick cinnamon. It has cinnamon-like flavor, but is stronger and sweeter, with a musky aroma. It can be used in desserts and rice dishes. Find it online and at most Asian grocery stores.

Cinnamon sticks (dalchini) These thin, smooth twirls of bark are creamy brown, and give a beautiful aroma to dishes both sweet and savory. There seems to be quite a confusion about cinnamon sticks and cassia bark, and they are used interchangeably in most kitchens. In the Indian kitchen we always use cassia bark, but because cinnamon is very similar it is also called by the same name. The Chinese refer to cassia as "true cinnamon."

Cloves (laung) The dried flower pods look like miniature black scepters (or like strange little nails). Their flavor is strong and distinct, and they should be used sparingly. Cloves create a warming sensation and are usually used in dishes alongside green cardamom. They're an important part of Indian chai (spiced tea) and are known for their antimicrobial properties.

Dried pomegranate seeds (anardana) These are the sun-dried seeds of the pomegranate fruit. When crushed, they gift a tangy sourness. They're used as a flavoring for dishes, to add that sweet-and-sour tang so loved by the Indian palate. Particularly important in street food and snacks, they're sprinkled over chaat dishes (savory snacks), used in the mixture for kebabs, and can be tasted in many chutneys.

Fennel seeds (saunf) Larger and flatter than cumin seeds and with a slightly green tint, fennel seeds have a distinct aniseed (or licorice-like) flavor. Highly aromatic, the whole seeds are used in pickles and chai. In India, fennel is chewed after meals as a breath freshener and as a digestive aid, relieving the feeling of being bloated.

Fenugreek seeds (methi) These look like little sharp yellow stones, and have a strong, bitter taste. They're generally tempered before use to intensify the flavor and aroma. Used commercially in curry powders, fenugreek seeds give off the very characteristic aroma that we tend to associate with curries. They're also used for pickling, a Punjabi yogurt-based dish called kharee, and are found in some spice blends, such as panch phoran.

Green cardamom (elachi) These small green pods each contain about 20 black seeds. They have a strong aroma and an intense, distinctly bittersweet flavor. They can be crushed or used whole, but only use a few, as they can be quite overpowering. Add them to savory dishes, most desserts, and chai.

Nigella seeds (kalonji, or kalvaji) These small black seeds have a similar taste to oregano, which is quite strong, so use sparingly. Kalonji seeds can be used as a milder substitute for pepper. Generally used in pickles and in naan bread. Medicinal applications include treatment of bowel and indigestion problems.

Mace (javitri) This is the outer coating of the nutmeg, and is usually sold as a powder or as blades. It has a strong and slightly sweet aroma, similar to nutmeg.

Mango powder (amchoor) This powder is made from the dried flesh of unripe green mangoes. The fibrous powder gives sauces and snacks a fruity tartness and is used in virtually the same way as lemon juice.

Poppy seeds (khas khas) Poppy seeds are oil seeds that come from the opium poppy, and they do contain very low levels of opiates. Harvested from the dried seed pods of the flower, they are highly nutritious and are used widely in kitchens around the world. Always tiny, the seeds can be white, black, or blue. The black seeds tend to be the most popular and are used in breads and puddings or as thickening agents. White poppy seeds are more commonly used in Indian cuisine. In the North, they thicken sauces and add a nutty texture to dishes. In Bengali cuisine, the seeds are an ingredient in their own right, and are used in dishes with potatoes, shrimp, and chicken. Don't worry if you can't find white poppy seeds, just substitute with black or brown varieties. My only word of caution is that for dishes such as korma—that is foods with a light-color sauce—using black seeds can make the dish too dark. As it's a thickening agent, I would be inclined to skip it rather than use black seeds.

Saffron (kesar) This precious spice is the stigma of a special autumn crocus, and is usually bought in strands. It is used for its golden color and very delicate flavor. It has a grassy aroma. Kesar is also used as a dye, as well as for a number of medicinal applications—it has recently been discovered to possess anticarcinogenic properties. When using kesar, you can heat and dry the strands for a few minutes and then grind them to a powder to intensify the color. The kesar is then steeped, or bloomed, in warm milk or water to draw out its warming flavor and hue.

The Essential Spice Blends

Different regions of India have specific spice blends that are used to add characteristic flavors to a dish—uniquely distinct, these mixes are emblematic of the areas they come from. Easily made in advance, these blends can be stored in airtight jars away from light and heat, and can be kept for up to six months.

Garam Masala

This is the iconic spice blend of North India and is usually added at the end of cooking to bring the dish together. If you want to make your own, here is my family blend. This will make about 3 tablespoons, and all you do is put the spices into a spice grinder and blend.

2 tablespoons cumin seeds

1 tablespoon coriander seeds

1 teaspoon black peppercorns

½ teaspoon carom seeds

5 cloves

4 green cardamom pods

2 bay leaves

2 black cardamom pods

1-inch (3-cm) piece cassia bark, broken into bits

Panch Phoran

This is a whole spice blend typically used in Bangladesh. Also a reliable pickling spice blend. I use this in my Indian Tomato Ketchup with Pickling Spices (page 168). You can make your own with equal measures of black mustard seeds, nigella seeds, fennel seeds, and cumin seeds, plus half the amount of fenugreek seeds.

Chaat Masala

Chaat masala is a tangy spice blend that is used for savory street-food snacks. For a tangy twist, many Indians will also sprinkle chaat masala atop fruit. The word chaat means "to lick," implying that it's a mouth-tingling blend.

1 tablespoon cumin seeds

1 tablespoon coriander seeds

1½ teaspoons fennel seeds

1 teaspoon whole black peppercorns

¼ teaspoon asafetida

½ tablespoon garam masala (opposite)

½ tablespoon dried mango powder (amchoor)

½ tablespoon black salt

1 teaspoon chili powder

⅛ teaspoon ground ginger

1. Put the cumin seeds, coriander seeds, fennel seeds, and black peppercorns in a small frying pan over low heat and dry roast for a few minutes until fragrant.

2. Add the asafetida and stir for a few moments.

3. Remove from the heat and leave to cool. Grind the combination in a spice grinder to a fine powder.

4. Add the remaining ingredients and grind again.

5. Store in an airtight jar away from heat and light for up to 6 months.

Proper Spice Storage

Storing your spices properly ensures that they will maintain their natural oils for longer. After all, it's those oils that heighten the flavor of your food, so preserving them is your main goal. Follow these simple rules.

- Keep your spices dry.
- Store them in an airtight container.
- Keep them in the dark.
- Store them away from a heat source.

Most Indian homes have an Indian spice tin—called a masala dabba—in their kitchen drawer because it's the best way to store your spices, keeping them fresh and all in one place. The masala dabba is a round, stainless steel tin with seven smaller tins inside of which you keep your precious spices. Each smaller tin has a lid to ensure spices are airtight and kept in the dark, and there's a large lid that covers the entire container, so everything stays in one place—practical and convenient. Plus there's a useful tiny spoon, perfect for spooning your spices into your dish. My tin contains ground chili powder, ground turmeric, mustard seeds, coriander seeds, cumin seeds, fenugreek seeds, and garam masala—seven key flavors!

Whole spices are at their best when used within 9 to 12 months, and ground spices within 6 to 12 months. But rather than going by dates on the package, use your senses.

Whole or Ground?

Spices are fruits, nuts, seeds, and even bark whose use enhances the flavor or color of food. They can give a cooling or a warming sensation, as well as adding sweetness or heat to dishes.

Whole spices are spices in their most natural form, being the way they grow; and ground spices are just those same spices ground to a fine powder. The ground varieties are easier to use, but in this processed form their natural oils are lost much more quickly.

My personal preference is to buy my spices whole and grind them as needed, either in my mortar and pestle (which I keep out on my work surface, rather than having the set stored away, so that I can grind spices quickly), or in my electric spice grinder. This said, if you are short of time during the week, there is nothing wrong with using a preground powder.

I always buy my chili powder and turmeric preground, as it's messy business grinding these spices. The oil from chiles gets into the air, making you cough and cry. I do, however, keep whole dried chiles in my pantry as well.

If the spices still smell good, look the color they should, and taste all right (yes, have a little taste), then they will still add the correct flavor to your dish. If you have green cardamom that is dry, gray, and has no aroma, then it's probably best to get rid of it. Very old spices can also become bitter and unpleasant in your food, so do test them and replace them if required.

MASALA DABBA Not only is the masala dabba a convenient and practical way to store spices, because there is no need to open up individual jars, but the compartment also looks attractive in the modern kitchen. Cooking equipped with a masala dabba makes you feel like a professional—giving you the much-needed confidence when you are cooking something different.

Dhal (Lentils and Beans)

Dhal is a word that means lentils or beans, and refers to both the ingredient itself and the final cooked dish. In India, dhal is a huge source of protein for much of the population, and dhal and rice is the simplest form of nutrition. Most Indian meals will include a dhal of some kind. Dhal can be eaten as a side dish for a larger meal or can be a simple meal eaten on its own with rice or bread and usually a wet dish, like a soup. There is a huge (and I mean *huge*) variety of lentils and beans that are used in Indian cuisine.

Lentils are usually associated with the flat variety. They grow in Asia and North Africa, in pods that contain two or three lentils inside each. Full of protein and carbohydrates, lentils are also a great source of calcium, phosphorous, B vitamins, and iron.

The wonderful thing about lentils is that there are so many different varieties and each one has its own texture, taste profile, and use. Lentils can also be mixed with other varieties to produce new flavors and dishes.

Beans are usually larger, and they also grow in pods in the summer months. Beans generally require a bit more cooking time than lentils.

With stovetop cooking, I recommend that certain whole beans and lentils be soaked overnight, but this step is not required when they are cooked in a slow cooker—except for kidney beans.

Dhal can be bought in a variety of forms, and surprisingly, the same lentil or bean in a different form can produce very different-tasting dishes.

Sabut: whole with the skin intact

Dhuli sabut: whole with the skin removed (dhuli means "washed")

Green Mung Beans

Chickpeas ▶

Split Yellow Pigeon Peas

Kidney Beans

Black Lentils

Brown Lentils

Split Gram

Yellow Mung Beans

Red Lentils

Chilka: split with the skin (the chilka) on

Dhuli: split with the skin removed

The cooking times vary significantly, because whole dhals with the skins intact will take much longer to cook than the other forms. Left whole, they are also more nutritious, but must be cooked thoroughly to ensure they can be properly digested.

Before cooking, make sure you sift through the dhal to remove any twigs or gravel. Then wash thoroughly in three or four changes of water to remove excess starch. Here's a short description of the types of dhal used for recipes in this book:

Black lentils (urid beans, black gram, sabut maa) These are black, oval lentils used across India. They break down in cooking to produce a rich-and-creamy lentil dish.

Brown lentils (sabut masoor) Dark-brown round lentils are hearty and wholesome, with a nutty flavor. They hold their shape well when cooked and produce a thick flavorsome dhal. When they are split and skinned, they are known as red or pink lentils (masoor).

Red lentils (masoor) Also known as pink lentils, they are the result of dehusking and splitting brown lentils. They cook fairly quickly and turn a lovely yellow color. These are one of my favorite lentils, and the dhal made with them is my go-to lentil dish because it has a delicious flavor that is light and fresh.

Chickpeas (channa, chole, sholay) With their wonderful homey flavor, these round beige legumes are used in a number of dishes in this book. In fact, they appear in many forms of Indian cooking. Black chickpeas (or kala channa), the second variety of chickpeas, are not as well known in the Western world. Kala channa are smaller and much darker. They are nutritious and very high in protein, but require much longer cooking times. They don't break down like other dhal, but do make a wonderful gravy when cooked.

Split gram (channa dhal) This is the black chickpea split and skinned, leaving a yellow legume. It's very hearty and adds a depth and warmth to dishes.

Green mung beans (green gram, green moong) These are small green legumes that cook quickly for a whole dhal. Cooked, they have a creamy consistency.

Yellow mung beans (yellow moong) When split and skinned, green mung beans end up a light-yellow color, and probably cook the fastest of all the dhals. This is a delicate legume that is easy on the tummy.

Split yellow pigeon peas (toor dhal, gungo beans, arhar dhal) These are split-and-skinned pigeon peas that are used a great deal in South Indian cooking. They are pale yellow in color. They cook down completely and give a nice thick consistency. They can be bought dry or with an oily coating that needs to be washed off before cooking.

Kidney beans (rajma) These are beautiful deep-purple beans. Now a word of warning: Kidney beans have a natural toxin in them called phytohaemagglutinin, or kidney-bean lectin, which can cause nausea and sickness, so it is very important to cook them thoroughly. Dried beans should be soaked overnight and then heated to the boiling point for at least 10 minutes; then change the water and place the beans in a slow cooker. If you slow cook kidney beans at a lower temperature without first soaking and boiling them, there is a risk that the toxin levels will increase.

Rice, Grains, and Flours

Rice and flour are the key staples of Indian cuisine, and are a regular part of each meal. In the South, every meal consists of rice cooked in one form or another, from plain rice to rice cakes (called idlis) to pilaus. In North India wheat is the main staple, so every meal would include roti or another form of bread. Other types of flour are also frequently used, such as gram (chickpea) and millet flours.

Basmati rice (chawal) When it comes to Indian food, basmati is the rice of choice. This long-grain rice is grown only in North India, and is known for its fragrance and delicate flavor. You should be able to find it in the supermarket—look in the ethnic-food aisle if it's not alongside the short-grain rice. When cooking rice, it's really important to wash it in several changes of water to get rid of the excess starch, so the grains elongate beautifully and you are left with individual fluffy rice. You'll find a recipe for cooking the perfect pot of basmati rice in your slow cooker on page 180.

Gram flour (besan) This pale-yellow flour is made by milling dried brown chickpeas. It is used in Indian, Middle Eastern, and some Asian cuisines. It's also gluten-free, which is a real bonus if you are gluten intolerant. If you can't find it in your supermarket, try the health-food store or go online.

This flour is a vital part of Indian cuisine—it's used to make batter, for spiced cakes and confections, and as a thickening agent. It's also a great stabilizer; when mixed into yogurt, it will stop it from breaking up. When using gram flour in a marinade or in a sauce, it's a really good idea to toast the flour in a dry frying pan (no oil required) first, as this removes the raw-flour taste and adds an earthy nuttiness. It needs to be toasted for about five minutes, until it releases a sweet aroma and turns a touch darker in color. Make sure you keep it moving in the pan to prevent burning—once toasted, immediately remove it from the hot pan.

Atta

Gram Flour ▶

Basmati Rice

Atta This is a whole-wheat flour made from the hard wheat that grows across the Indian subcontinent. It is used for many Indian flatbreads, including roti, poori, and paratha. If you can't find atta, a good substitute can be made by mixing half whole-wheat flour and half white flour.

Fresh Ingredients and Produce

Indian food is all about keeping things fresh, and produce is an important part of that. Most of the items listed are available in supermarkets. Other items are a little more specialized and can be purchased online or from smaller local Indian or Asian grocery stores. You can even try growing some of these in your garden—or in your home kitchen, as coriander, mint, and curry leaves can be grown indoors.

Curry leaves (kari patha) Curry leaves are small, pointed, fragrant, dark-green leaves from the curry plant, which is a shrub that grows in India and Sri Lanka. The leaves are highly aromatic and iconic in South Indian cooking, where they are used in all types of dishes, from dhals to meat curries. Please be aware that curry powder is not the powdered form of these leaves. Curry powder is a spice blend that includes chile, turmeric, cumin, and fenugreek, and is supposed to be everything you need for a curry in one blend.

I prefer to use the fresh leaves rather than the dried ones, as unprocessed they have a much more pungent flavor, but if you are unable to find fresh leaves, dried ones will do—though you may need to increase the amount you use. If you cannot find these leaves then I would omit them from the recipe, as there isn't really any substitute.

Chiles (mirch) I could easily dedicate an entire chapter just to chiles, but most important to know is that Indian foods use chiles in many different ways. Fresh green chiles (hari mirch), usually a Thai or serrano, are used during the cooking process to add heat, freshness, and flavor. Dried red chiles (lal mirch), such as dried Kashmiri or cayenne, are treated as a whole spice and are tempered in oil at the start of the cooking process.

How you treat your chile will determine how much heat you get. Put them in whole and you will get the flavor and a little heat; chop them finely and you will get the full heat and flavor. The heat sits on the inside membrane, so when you scrape out the seeds you reduce some of the heat. Personally, I think slicing the chile in half to scrape out the seeds is a real hassle—you end up with the chile all over your fingers, and with spicy aromas floating around in the air you're likely to rub your eyes, which is not a pleasant experience. I recommend that if you don't want the dish to be too hot, just chop up half a chile and save the other half for another dish.

Chili powder is used for color and to add a bit more punch. Always use a combination of the powder and fresh chiles in a dish. Too much chili powder will give a dry, unpleasant heat.

Always cook to your taste and remember that over time your palate can evolve and learn to enjoy the heat.

Coriander (thania or dhania) Fresh coriander (called "cilantro" in North America) is a delicate herb with beautiful, perfumed flat leaves that give a delicate freshness to every dish. The flavor is completely different from that of coriander seeds, so do not substitute one for the other. Temperature will also diminish the fragrance of fresh coriander leaves, so be mindful to add the ingredient immediately before serving.

More than just a simple garnish, coriander is a vital part of many Indian foods—it's about enhancing the look and flavor of your final dish.

The stalks are very underrated. Don't throw them away. Instead, chop them up very finely and add them during the cooking process to enhance the sauce with a wonderful aromatic flavor.

Garlic (lasan) A member of the onion family, garlic has a unique flavor that is strong and quite harsh when raw. Garlic tends to go hand in hand with onions, and in many cuisines they are cooked together, along with tomatoes, to produce a base sauce—from Italian tomato sauces to Indian masala bases to Mexican chilies. When cooked, the sharp flavor of garlic mellows and sweetens.

Peeled garlic can be chopped, crushed, sliced, minced, or even used whole. Garlic lasts for ages in the refrigerator, but you can also freeze it—or mince and freeze it in ice cube trays, for easy use later.

European chefs recommend removing the green germ from the middle of a garlic clove, as this center can cause indigestion. But it doesn't seem to be a problem in Indian cooking because the garlic is cooked for so long.

Garlic has amazing health benefits, too. If you have the sniffles, dishes like rasam (South Indian Tomato and Pepper Soup, page 42) will sort you right out. Plus, garlic also offers cardiovascular health advantages.

Ginger root (athrak) An absolute essential ingredient of Indian cooking, fresh ginger sits alongside onions and garlic as the third musketeer for Indian masala sauces. Root ginger has a characteristically fresh and almost citruslike aroma. It adds a distinct brightness, a little spicy heat, and some warmth. It can be used in both savory and sweet dishes. Dry ground-ginger powder isn't a substitute for fresh ginger. I usually grate any leftover fresh ginger I have and freeze it in ice cube trays, and then pop out a cube when needed.

Tamarind

Jaggery

Garlic

Onions

Coriander

Chilies

Rose Water

Ginger Root

Onions

Pandan Water

Mint

Curry Leaves

Ginger is known to have many beneficial health properties, such as being a natural remedy for colds and headaches, not to mention its known blood-thinning and cholesterol-reducing properties.

Jaggery (gur) This is very dark unrefined cane sugar, with a fudge-like consistency. Muscovado sugar, or any dark-brown sugar, is a good substitute if you can't find jaggery.

Mint (pudina) Mint has a fresh, aromatic, and sweet taste with a cooling after-sensation. It is used in cooking to give that sought-after freshness, especially in sauces and chutneys. Mint is also known as a home remedy for relieving stomach pains and indigestion.

Onions (gunda and pyaz) There is no getting away from onions—Indian food requires loads of them. Yellow onions (gunda) and red onions (pyaz) are the best choices for Indian dishes, as they offer the right pungency. I also like to use shallots for certain dishes. Interestingly, for religious reasons some Indian communities do not consume onions at all, so they use asafetida powder to achieve the same level of pungency.

Pandan water (kewra) Also called screwpine or kewra water, this unique-smelling liquid is distilled from the flower of the pandan tree. It's typically used in biryanis, drinks, and desserts to add fragrance. It can be purchased online and is fairly inexpensive. Kewra usually keeps for a few months at room temperature.

Rose water (gulaab jal) This distinctive rose-perfumed water is very much an Indian and Middle Eastern ingredient. A by-product of rose-oil production, the substance also has applications in the cosmetics industry. It's used to fragrance desserts such as kulfi (Indian ice cream) and sweets such as Turkish delight, and is also an ingredient in some of the most decadent savory dishes like biryanis. Available online and sometimes in confectionary or cake shops, rose water keeps for a few months in your cupboard.

Tamarind (imlee) Tamarind is the ripened pulp of a fruit of a native Indian shade tree. The fruit is long, with a similar shape to a butternut squash, is dark brown, and has large seeds. It is usually bought in solid blocks of pulp, which you soak in warm water and break down to make tamarind water or paste. It has a unique fruity and sour taste, and is used mainly in chutneys and pickles. It also has natural laxative properties.

It can be bought online in blocks, as a paste in jars, or as a concentrate—and it stores safely in the refrigerator for at least a few months. I would highly recommend steering away from purchasing the concentrate, as it's very thick and black, which can make your dishes look dark and unappetizing.

To make the tamarind pulp, place 2 to 4 tablespoons of the solid tamarind block into a large bowl and cover it with boiling water. Leave it to soften for about 10 to 15 minutes.

Using a fork, mash the pulp—by doing this the flavor will dissolve into the water. Push the mixture through a sieve to remove the stones and fibrous material. Retain the pulp. (You can repeat this process with the same tamarind to get more from it.)

Oils

I use different oils for different dishes, depending on where the dish comes from or what flavor profile I am looking to achieve. My oil of choice is rapeseed, because it's light and fresh and can be used both at high temperatures as well as in cold dishes. I only use olive oil for salads and dressings. For South Indian–style dishes, I rely on coconut oil, and mustard oil is amazing for vegetables and fish.

All these oils will be easy to find—if not in your supermarket, look in the organic market or health-food store. All can be stored at room temperature in sealed containers, away from direct sunlight. Coconut oil can be left for up to two years, mustard oil keeps for about six months, and rapeseed oil can be kept for many months.

Coconut oil This is a white oil extracted from the coconut. It solidifies at cooler temperatures (though in the wintertime even room temperatures can stiffen it) and remains in liquid form at higher temperatures. It is a stable oil at high temperatures, so it's a good choice for high-heat cooking. In Indian food, it's mainly used in South Indian cuisine, which is the region where coconuts abound. Coconut oil also has cosmetic applications, serving as a moisturizer and a nourishing hair oil.

Ghee Ghee is primarily used in North Indian cooking, adding richness and wonderful aromas. Ghee is clarified butter, which means it has been heated to remove the milk proteins, helping prevent the substance from going rancid, a property very important in the tropical climate of India. It can be stored at room temperature for many months. Heating butter to make ghee also caramelizes the sugars, resulting in a subtle nutty flavor.

Ghee not only tastes great but is also excellent to cook with, as it can withstand high temperatures. When chilled, ghee turns from a golden liquid to a solid grainy texture, whose roughness smooths out as soon as ghee is reheated.

You can buy ghee online—or make it yourself: Gently heat butter until it froths. Skim the froth off and leave it to simmer until the sugars caramelize. Remove from the heat and leave it to settle, then pour off the golden liquid (the ghee), leaving the brown sediment at the bottom. Ghee will keep for up to 12 months at room temperature. Be mindful not to introduce contaminants into your ghee with unclean spoons.

A good substitute is using half butter and half oil. Although it's a great oil to use, be aware that it is still saturated fat—so use sparingly.

Ghee

Rapeseed Oil

Coconut Oil

Mustard Oil

Mustard oil Used in North and East Indian cooking, mustard oil has a distinctly pungent flavor. Used in particular to cook vegetable dishes, such as okra and green beans, it also works really well with fish dishes—no matter the use, its natural potency enhances dishes with a delicious bite. Please be aware that mustard oil has high levels of uric acid, which can be a problem for some people.

Rapeseed oil This is my oil of choice when it comes to Indian food. Light and fresh, rapeseed oil has a higher smoking point than other oils, which means it doesn't oxidize and become unhealthy for us to use during cooking.

Essential Kitchen Tools

These key pieces of equipment will make life in the kitchen a bit easier. Included are also a few items required for completing the Indian kitchen.

Immersion blender, blender, or food processor. Slow-cooker cooking requires a blender of some kind to help blend onions, ginger, garlic, and tomatoes. Blending is essential for fusing soups and for getting smooth sauces. I find an immersion blender most convenient for finishing, so there are thick and luxurious sauces right in the cooker.

Mortar and pestle. Using whole spices makes a mortar-and-pestle set a must-have. In the Indian kitchen you will regularly grind individual spices and mince or mash ingredients such as ginger and garlic. My advice is to always keep your mortar and pestle accessible, which will encourage you to use it. If you store the set out of sight in a cupboard, you will find getting it out to be a hassle. Plus, I do think that this grinder's rustic esthetic looks great in a modern kitchen.

Spice grinder. These are perfect for making spice blends such as garam masala or ginger-and-garlic pastes. An electric coffee grinder makes an excellent spice grinder, but if you are a regular coffee drinker, get a dedicated grinder for your spices. You don't want coffee oils in your spices—or spice oils in your coffee.

Tava. This is a concave cast-iron griddle pan that you place directly on the stovetop. Because the griddle is thin, the temperature is easily controllable. If you want to make Indian flatbreads, a tava is a must. It is also excellent for toasting spices, but it's also great for other dishes, too. I quite often cook burgers and omelets on mine.

Mortar and Pestle ▶

◀ Spice Grinder

Tava

To Slow Cook or Not to Slow Cook?

Food items like tough cuts of meat are perfect for cooking in a slow cooker. But there are some foods that just don't cook slowly well. Here is a helpful list of some of these foods, as well as a few tips and tricks to make do while still taking full advantage of your slow cooker.

Frozen Food: Always make sure that frozen food is fully defrosted before cooking in a slow cooker, as it will take too long for it to reach a safe temperature.

Seafood: Most seafood takes minutes to cook and can become rubbery if cooked for too long. Fish and shellfish are also expensive, so it's best to either focus on meat in your slow cooker or to add the seafood to your dish toward the end of the cooking time.

Delicate vegetables: Ingredients such as asparagus and peas should either be added at the end or cooked separately as a side dish, because cooking them for a long time means they will lose their vibrant, delicate flavors. They will also turn mushy, resulting in an unpleasant texture.

Delicate herbs: These should really be added toward the end of cooking to ensure you get their full flavor. Heat will diminish their aromatics.

Yogurt and dairy products: Low-fat dairy products do not work in a slow cooker because they separate easily—which is also true of full-fat dairy products—leaving an unpleasant lumpy consistency when cooked for too long. If you do want to use yogurt, you will need to mix it with something like gram flour to stabilize it. You can also stir it in at the end of the cooking process.

Ginger Soup *page 48*

Chapter Three

Soups

South Indian Tomato and Pepper Soup

Rasam

⚙ QUICK PREP Ⓥ VEGAN | SERVES 6
PREP TIME: 5 MINUTES | COOK TIME: 6 HOURS ON LOW OR 3 TO 4 HOURS ON HIGH

I was introduced to rasam on a cold winter morning by the South Indian chef at a restaurant I was then working at. I love consommé-style soups, which have an intense flavor but are essentially just broth. The rasam he made for me included all of the ingredients listed here, except the dhal, thrown into a pot and cooked, then blended and sieved. I have never had anything so intense before or since. When I remember back, I can literally feel the heat from the rasam warming my whole body, and on that cold morning the sensation was just perfect. For this recipe I have added split yellow pigeon peas to give the dish a little more body.

6⅓ cups (1½ liters) hot water

⅓ cup split yellow pigeon peas (toor dhal)

1 tablespoon tamarind paste

1 heaped teaspoon black peppercorns

1 heaped teaspoon cumin seeds

1 teaspoon turmeric

20 curry leaves

6 tomatoes, roughly chopped

2 dried red chiles

4 garlic cloves, roughly chopped

4-inch (10-cm) piece fresh ginger, roughly chopped

Handful coriander stalks, finely chopped

Coriander leaves to garnish

1. Place all of the ingredients in the slow cooker. Cover and cook on low for 6 hours, or on high for 3 to 4 hours.

2. Use an immersion blender, or regular blender, to make a fine purée.

3. Taste and add a little more salt, if required.

4. Garnish with coriander leaves to serve.

EASY ADJUSTMENT: If preferred, you can make this dish less spicy by reducing the amount of black pepper and chiles. The recipe can also be divided in half and cooked in a smaller 3½-quart (3½-liter) slow cooker.

Spiced Butternut Squash Soup with Coconut Cream

Nariyal Kuddu Shorba

VEGETARIAN | SERVES 6

PREP TIME: 15 MINUTES | COOK TIME: 6 HOURS ON LOW OR 3 HOURS ON HIGH

You can't really get butternut squash in India—although people there do have access to pumpkins—so this is not necessarily the most traditional of Indian dishes. But this vegetable soup is perfectly balanced, with warming cumin seeds and the chile counteracting the sweetness of the coconut cream. It's all wrapped up in a vivid-orange soup that is so inviting. Serve with some warmed Naan (page 184). If it's a cuddle in a bowl you are looking for, then this soup will certainly deliver. Make sure you buy canned coconut cream, which is much thicker than coconut milk.

1 tablespoon coconut oil

1 teaspoon cumin seeds

3 garlic cloves, chopped finely

2 butternut squash, peeled, seeded, and chopped into chunks

2 red onions, peeled and chopped

2-inch (5-cm) piece fresh ginger, grated

2 to 3 fresh red chiles, chopped (keep some for garnish)

4 cups (1 liter) water or vegetable stock

⅓ cup (100 mL) coconut cream

Salt to taste

1. Preheat the slow cooker on high.

2. Heat the coconut oil in a frying pan (or in the slow cooker if you have a sear setting) and add the cumin seeds. As soon as they release their aroma, add the garlic and fry for 1 minute.

3. Add the butternut squash, onions, ginger, and chiles.

4. Add the stock, cover, and cook on low for 6 hours, or on high for 3 hours.

5. Using an immersion or regular blender, purée the soup until it's smooth and thick.

6. Pour in the coconut cream and let cook for another 10 minutes on high.

7. Check the seasoning and consistency of the soup. If it's too thick, add a little hot water.

8. Pour into bowls and top with a swirl of coconut cream and a chopped chile to garnish.

SIMPLE SUBSTITUTION: Sweet potatoes or pumpkin can be used in the same quantities instead of butternut squash, if you prefer.

Spicy Chicken Soup
Masala Murgh Thari

SERVES 6

PREP TIME: 15 MINUTES | COOK TIME: 6 HOURS ON LOW OR 3 HOURS ON HIGH

I love this dish because it's essentially a mouth-tingling chicken-curry gravy (that's the thari part) filled with delicious pieces of succulent chicken. The gravy is packed with flavor and the spices will ward off any signs of a cold. I think for a delicious broth the bones add some hearty goodness (though if you prefer, cook with thighs that are off the bone)—a filling meal that cooks easily in a slow cooker.

4 to 5 chicken thighs, skinned and trimmed, on the bone

½ teaspoon turmeric

½ teaspoon sea salt, plus more for seasoning

½-inch (1-cm) piece cassia bark

2 cloves

2 teaspoons coriander seeds

½ teaspoon black peppercorns

2 dried red chiles

1 teaspoon white poppy seeds (or black poppy seeds)

2 teaspoons cumin seeds, divided

2-inch (5-cm) piece fresh ginger

3 garlic cloves

3 to 4 small shallots, cut into chunks

1 tablespoon rapeseed oil

1 teaspoon mustard seeds

20 curry leaves

Handful fresh coriander stems, chopped (chop and save the leaves for the garnish)

1 teaspoon Kashmiri chili powder

1 cup canned tomatoes, blended

4 cups (1 liter) hot water

½ teaspoon Garam Masala (page 23)

2 tablespoons lemon juice

1. Preheat the slow cooker on high.

2. Rub the chicken thighs with turmeric and salt, and set aside.

3. Put the cassia bark, cloves, coriander seeds, black peppercorns, red chiles, poppy seeds, and 1 teaspoon of cumin seeds into a spice grinder and grind to a powder.

4. In a food processor or blender, add the ginger, garlic, and shallots and grind. Add the ground spices and a splash of water, and process to make a paste.

5. Heat the oil in a frying pan on medium-high (or in the slow cooker if you have a sear setting) and add the mustard seeds and remaining 1 teaspoon of cumin seeds. Once they are sizzling, add the curry leaves and the spice-ginger-garlic paste. Stir and cook for about 5 to 6 minutes.

6. Empty the contents into the slow cooker. Add the chicken thighs, coriander stems, chili powder, tomatoes, and water. Season with salt. Cover and cook for 6 hours on low, or for 3 hours on high.

7. Once cooked through, either shred the chicken and remove the bones or serve on the bone.

8. Add the chopped coriander leaves, garam masala, and a squeeze of lemon juice, and serve in bowls.

SIMPLE SUBSTITUTION: You can also cook this with an equal amount of lamb, if you prefer.

Fennel and Tomato Soup
Saunf Tomatar Shorba

⚙ QUICK PREP Ⓥ VEGAN | SERVES 6
PREP TIME: 10 MINUTES | **COOK TIME: 4 HOURS ON LOW OR 2 HOURS ON HIGH**

This shorba has a gentle aniseed flavor from the fennel seed, which works beautifully with the freshness of the ripe tomatoes. It's a perfect dish for a slow cooker, as the time allows the spices to infuse the soup. If you are short on time, skip the tempering and just throw everything into the slow cooker.

2 tablespoons rapeseed oil

2 teaspoons fennel seeds

5 garlic cloves, sliced

2 fresh green chiles

1 teaspoon salt

1 pound (500 g) ripe tomatoes, roughly chopped

Handful fresh coriander stems, roughly chopped

3 cups (750 mL) hot water

1 teaspoon fennel seeds, roasted and roughly crushed, for garnish

1. Preheat the slow cooker on high.

2. Heat the oil in a frying pan (or in the slow cooker if you have a sear setting) and add the fennel seeds. When they are sizzling, add the garlic and cook until it is just brown. Pour everything into the slow cooker.

3. Throw in the whole green chiles and the salt.

4. Add the chopped tomatoes, coriander stems, and water.

5. Cook on low for 4 hours, or on high for 2 hours.

6. Using an immersion or regular blender, purée until smooth.

7. Pour into serving bowls and serve topped with a few toasted fennel seeds.

EASY ADJUSTMENT: If you prefer a thicker soup, remove the cover and cook on high for the last 30 minutes. If you prefer it thinner, add some boiling water and adjust the seasoning in the last 30 minutes.

Yellow Mung Bean Soup with Lime

Dhuli Moong Dhal Shorba

⏱ QUICK PREP 🌿 VEGETARIAN | SERVES 6
PREP TIME: 10 MINUTES | COOK TIME: 4 HOURS ON LOW OR 2 HOURS ON HIGH

Mung beans are a great little legume that is easy to digest—and cooking the beans in the slow cooker is an effortless option. A squeeze of lime right at the end of cooking adds a bright dimension, making the dish sublime. For a vegan variation, use vegetable oil instead of ghee.

1 tablespoon ghee or vegetable oil

1 teaspoon cumin seeds

2 garlic cloves, chopped

2 cups yellow mung beans, washed

4 cups (1 liter) water

1 teaspoon salt

2 tomatoes, finely chopped

1 teaspoon freshly grated ginger

1 teaspoon turmeric

1 fresh green chile, finely chopped

Juice of 1 lime

1 teaspoon Garam Masala (page 23)

Chopped coriander leaves, to garnish

1. Preheat the slow cooker on high.

2. Heat the ghee in a frying pan (or in the slow cooker if you have a sear setting) and add the cumin seeds. As soon as they release their fragrance, add the chopped garlic until it just starts to turn golden brown.

3. Pour everything into the slow cooker and add the mung beans, water, salt, chopped tomatoes, grated ginger, turmeric, and chopped chile.

4. Cook on low for 4 hours, or on high for 2 hours. Check that the beans are soft and cooked through.

5. Using an immersion or regular blender, purée the dhal until it's smooth. Check the seasonings, and if it's too thick add a little hot water.

6. Squeeze in the lime juice, add the garam masala, and stir.

7. Top with the fresh coriander leaves and serve.

TECHNIQUE TIP: It's best to add the lime juice just before you serve, as it freshens and lightens the soup.

Ginger Soup

Athrak Shorba

QUICK PREP | VEGAN | SERVES 6

PREP TIME: 10 MINUTES | COOK TIME: 4 HOURS ON LOW OR 2 HOURS ON HIGH

This is an old family favorite, and like the rasam, it has a spicy kick. Whenever my mum was feeling a bit under the weather, she would throw together this ginger soup to fill her with healing spices, and the concoction always got her back on her feet. She would break her roti into small pieces and soak it in the soup for a light, spicy, and nutritious meal.

4-inch (10-cm) piece fresh ginger, roughly chopped, plus julienned for garnish

2 fresh green chiles, chopped

6 cloves of garlic

1 (14-ounce/400-g) can tomatoes

2 cups (500 mL) water

1 tablespoon rapeseed oil

2 teaspoons cumin seeds

1 teaspoon salt

½ teaspoon turmeric

1 heaped teaspoon Garam Masala (page 23)

Handful fresh coriander leaves, chopped, for garnish

1. Preheat the slow cooker on high.

2. In a blender, add the ginger, chiles, garlic, tomatoes, and water, and purée to a paste. Set aside.

3. Heat the oil in a frying pan (or in the slow cooker if you have a sear setting) and add the cumin seeds. Cook until they are fragrant, then pour into the slow cooker along with the blended paste. Add the salt, turmeric, and garam masala.

4. Cover and cook on low for 4 hours, or on high for 2 hours.

5. Check the seasonings and adjust if required. Top with the julienned ginger and coriander leaves, and serve.

- -

PORTION TIP: This soup is perfect to serve as a little appetizer or as an amuse-bouche before an Indian dinner party. As a heartier course, serve with Whole-Wheat Flatbread (page 181).

Garlic and Mushroom Soup

Lansooni Khumb Shorba

⚙ QUICK PREP ◔ VEGETARIAN | SERVES 6

PREP TIME: 5 MINUTES | COOK TIME: 4 HOURS ON LOW OR 2 HOURS ON HIGH

I love mushrooms and I love garlic, and we all know that garlic and mushrooms are a classic combination. In this shorba I have added a little chile and some garam masala to bring to life the Indian side of the dish: a hearty soup with the full-profile flavor of mushrooms. Please feel free to substitute with other types of mushrooms, or a selection of mushrooms.

1 tablespoon rapeseed oil

10 garlic cloves, chopped

3 teaspoons butter

3 teaspoons cornstarch

1¾ pounds (800 g) chestnut or cremini mushrooms, quartered

Sea salt

Freshly ground black pepper

4 cups (1 liter) hot water

1 teaspoon Garam Masala (page 23)

1 teaspoon chili powder

Cream, for garnish (optional)

1. Preheat the slow cooker on high.

2. Heat the oil in a frying pan (or in the slow cooker if you have a sear setting) and toast the garlic until it starts to just brown. Add the butter and sprinkle in the cornstarch.

3. Pour everything into the slow cooker. Add the quartered mushrooms and season with salt and pepper. Pour in the hot water and give the mixture a good stir.

4. Cover and cook on low for 4 hours, or on high for 2 hours.

5. Using an immersion or regular blender, purée the soup until smooth. Then stir in the garam masala and chili powder.

6. Check the seasoning and adjust if required.

7. Pour into bowls and top with a little cream, if you want to, just before serving.

Cumin and Cauliflower Soup

Jeera Gobi Shorba

QUICK PREP | VEGAN | SERVES 6

PREP TIME: 12 MINUTES | COOK TIME: 4 HOURS ON LOW OR 2 HOURS ON HIGH

Cauliflower is very underrated, but this cabbage is starting to make a comeback in popularity—which is fantastic! Cauliflower is used a lot in Indian cooking, and I think it has a delicious flavor that works wonderfully well as a soup, especially with the additional warming aromatics of cumin. This dish is simple and full of warmth, which is what Indian soups are all about.

2 tablespoons rapeseed oil

1 bay leaf

2 teaspoons cumin seeds

5 garlic cloves, sliced

2 fresh green chiles

1 head of cauliflower, chopped

1 teaspoon sea salt

4 cups (1 liter) hot water

1. Preheat the slow cooker on high.

2. Heat the oil in a frying pan (or in the slow cooker if you have a sear setting) and add the bay leaf and the cumin seeds. When they are aromatic, stir in the garlic and sauté until it just browns. Pour the whole thing into the slow cooker.

3. Roughly chop the chiles and add them to the slow cooker, along with the chopped cauliflower, salt, and water.

4. Cover and cook on low for 4 hours, or on high for 2 hours.

5. Remove the bay leaf. Using an immersion or regular blender, purée the soup until it's smooth. Check the seasonings and adjust if required.

6. To garnish, dry-fry a few cumin seeds until fragrant, about 1 minute. Serve in small bowls and top with a sprinkling of roasted cumin.

- -

PORTION TIP: This recipe can easily be doubled—and if you do make enough for another day, the soup freezes well (up to 1 month).

Spicy Lamb Soup

Shorba Bakree

QUICK PREP | SERVES 6

PREP TIME: 12 MINUTES | COOK TIME: 6 HOURS ON LOW OR 4 HOURS ON HIGH

The idea of a lamb soup may sound a little unusual, but this shorba is from Kashmir, a region in India where they love their lamb. It's meaty and full of flavor, plus it's super easy to cook in a slow cooker. I think the mint makes it even more special, so do give the herb a try. And if you're feeling adventurous (and if you can get your hands on some), go for goat meat, because it's leaner than lamb. But if you use lamb, make sure you carefully trim off the fat.

1 pound (500 g) trimmed, boneless lamb neck or goat meat, cut into ¾-inch chunks

1 teaspoon salt

8½ cups hot water

1 teaspoon ghee

1 onion, sliced

½ teaspoon black pepper

2 fresh green chiles, chopped

Handful fresh coriander leaves, chopped

Handful fresh mint leaves, chopped

Lime juice

1. Preheat the slow cooker on high.

2. Spray a little nonstick cooking spray inside and very quickly sear the meat.

3. Turn the cooker to low, and add the salt and the hot water. Cover and cook on low for 6 hours, or on high for 4 hours.

4. When the lamb is tender, heat the ghee in a frying pan and add the onions. Sauté them for about 5 minutes, until they brown. Add them to the slow cooker with the black pepper, green chiles, coriander leaves, mint, and a squeeze of lime. Mix into the soup and leave to heat through for 15 minutes.

5. Check the seasonings and serve.

INGREDIENT TIP: Goat meat is used a lot in Indian cooking, although it's called lamb in India. Goat meat is perfect to cook in a slow cooker because the low-and-slow method allows flavors to penetrate the meat. And because it is not as fatty as lamb, the resulting goat dish is much lighter and healthier.

Saffron Rice *page 54*

Rice Dishes

Saffron Rice

Zafrani Pilau

🌸 **QUICK PREP** ⏱ **VEGETARIAN | SERVES 6**

PREP TIME: 10 MINUTES | COOK TIME: 1½ TO 2 HOURS ON HIGH

This is a simple yet elegant dish that I cooked daily at the restaurant I worked at. Slightly richer than a Plain Basmati Rice (page 180), this dish is made decadent by adding cream and butter. Saffron is generally a more expensive pantry item, making this rice dish perfect for special events or occasions. The saffron gives the amazing golden sprinkling that makes this dish stand out.

1⅓ cups basmati rice

Pinch saffron

1 tablespoon vegetable oil

1 teaspoon cumin seeds

3⅓ cups (800 mL) hot water

1 teaspoon salt

1 tablespoon butter

4 tablespoons (50 mL) cream

1. Wash the rice in two or three changes of water until the water runs clear. Then leave it to soak in warm water while you prep the rest of the dish.

2. Grind a few threads of saffron in a mortar and pestle. Add 2 tablespoons of hot water and stir.

3. Heat the slow cooker to high and add the oil. Add the cumin seeds and let them toast.

4. Pour the boiling water, salt, butter, and cream into the slow cooker. Strain the soaked rice and add to the slow cooker.

5. Stir and cover with the lid. Cook on high for 1½ to 2 hours. Halfway through the cooking, very gently stir the rice.

6. Turn off the cooker and sprinkle in the saffron water. Let it stand with the lid open for 5 to 10 minutes. Then toss the rice with a fork.

TECHNIQUE TIP: The longer you soak the rice, the less cooking time the dish requires.

Green Mung Beans with Rice

Moongi Khichdi

 VEGAN | SERVES 6

PREP TIME: 40 MINUTES, INCLUDING SOAKING THE BEANS | COOK TIME: 2 TO 3 HOURS ON LOW OR 1 TO 2 HOURS ON HIGH

Khichdi is a basic dish made simply with dhal and rice. Very popular in India, the meal is quick and cheap. The slow cooker is all about comfort food and khichdi is the perfect dish to cook in it, making an already simple dish even easier. It can be made with lots of different types of dhal, but the most common is moong dhal. Khichdi can be made to be thick or runny, depending on your mood—and because it's an easy dhal to digest, the meal is an effective remedy served to people who are unwell.

1 cup green mung beans

1⅓ cups Plain Basmati Rice (page 180)

4 cups (1 liter) hot water

2 tablespoons rapeseed oil

2 onions, peeled and sliced

2½-inch (6-cm) piece fresh ginger, grated

2 tomatoes, diced

3 fresh green chiles, finely chopped

1 teaspoon turmeric

1 teaspoon salt

2 teaspoons cumin seeds

1 teaspoon Garam Masala (page 23)

Handful fresh coriander leaves, chopped

1. Wash the green mung beans and soak them for 30 to 40 minutes. Wash the rice in a few changes of water until the water runs clear, and soak for about 10 minutes.

2. Heat the slow cooker to high and pour in the boiling water with the green mung beans.

3. Add the oil, onions, ginger, tomatoes, chiles, turmeric, salt, and cumin seeds, and stir.

4. Add the rice and cover the slow cooker. Cover and cook for 2 to 3 hours on low, or for 1 to 2 hours on high.

5. When you are ready to serve, add the garam masala and fresh coriander leaves.

INGREDIENT TIP: I like to use whole green mung beans (rather than the split and skinned yellow ones) in the khichdi because they have a light flavor but still hold some texture.

Spiced Rice with Smoked Fish

Kedgeree

SERVES 6

PREP TIME: 20 MINUTES | COOK TIME: 3 HOURS ON HIGH

This is a beautiful example of food evolution from khichdi, the poor man's cheap sustenance of beans and rice, to kedgeree, a wealthy man's brunch dish filled with protein, flavor, and a few spices to set it all off. I use haddock, but any smoked fish should be fine—pollock, cod, whitefish, or even salmon. Typically, seafood is not ideal for the slow cooker as cooking fish low and slow can result in chewy and rubbery meat. However, follow the tip on the next page and you'll have a perfect dish ready by supper.

2 cups basmati rice

1 tablespoon ghee

2 teaspoons mustard seeds

2 teaspoons cumin seeds, ground

2-inch (5-cm) piece fresh ginger, grated

2 garlic cloves, finely chopped

2 fresh bay leaves

2 fresh red chiles, finely chopped

1 bunch scallions, finely chopped

1 teaspoon turmeric

2 tomatoes, finely chopped

Sea salt

3¾ cups (900 mL) hot water

10 ounces (300 g) smoked fish fillets

3 large eggs

2 handfuls fresh coriander leaves, chopped

Juice of 1 lemon

1. Wash the rice and soak for 10 minutes.

2. Heat the ghee in a frying pan (or in the slow cooker if you have a sear setting). Add the mustard seeds and cook until they pop. Then add the cumin seeds. Once fragrant (a few seconds), add the ginger, garlic, bay leaves, chiles, scallions, turmeric, tomatoes and season with salt. Cook for 5 minutes.

3. Add the rice and hot water. Place the fish on top, skin-side down, and cook on high for 3 hours.

4. On the stovetop, hard boil the eggs, and set aside.

5. After cooking for 3 hours, gently lift the fish out and remove the skin and bones.

6. When you are ready to eat, flake the fish into the rice, add the coriander leaves and lemon juice, and fold through.

7. Peel the shells from the eggs, slice into quarters, and arrange on top of the rice, and serve.

TECHNIQUE TIP: When cooking fish, I recommend setting the slow cooker on high, because a longer cook time on low will make the fish rubbery.

Mixed Vegetable Pilau

Sabji Pilau

 QUICK PREP · VEGAN | SERVES 6

PREP TIME: 10 MINUTES | **COOK TIME: 3 HOURS ON LOW OR 1½ HOURS ON HIGH, PLUS 20 MINUTES TO STEAM**

What's the difference between a pilau and a biryani? A biryani is a layered rice dish; a pilau is prepared by cooking and mixing the rice and masala together. Packed full of complex flavor, pilau is a great one-pot dish. It's easily a family favorite—and leftovers make a fantastic lunch for the following day.

1½ cups basmati rice, washed

1 tablespoon rapeseed oil

2 bay leaves

2-inch (5-cm) piece cassia bark

1 tablespoon black peppercorns

1 tablespoon cumin seeds

1 tablespoon coriander seeds

4 green cardamom pods

2 black cardamom pods

3 cloves

2 medium onions, chopped

1 teaspoon salt

1 tablespoon freshly grated ginger

1 garlic clove, chopped

2 fresh green chiles, chopped

1 teaspoon turmeric

Handful mint leaves, chopped

Handful fresh coriander leaves, chopped

2½ cups (600 mL) hot water

12 ounces (350 g) frozen mixed vegetables, thawed

1. Wash the rice in a few changes of water until the water runs clear. Soak the rice in warm water for 10 minutes.

2. Heat the oil in a frying pan (or in the slow cooker if you have a sear setting). Add the bay leaves, cassia bark, peppercorns, cumin and coriander seeds, green and black cardamom pods, and cloves. Sauté for 2 minutes until the spices become aromatic.

3. Add the chopped onions and cook for about 5 minutes, until soft. Stir in the salt with the ginger, garlic, green chiles, turmeric, mint, and coriander leaves.

4. Add everything to the slow cooker. Then add the drained rice and hot water. Stir through gently.

5. Cover the slow cooker and cook on high for 1½ hours, or 3 hours on low. Stir the rice once during the cooking time.

6. Switch the cooker to the warming function, add the mixed vegetables, and stir through gently. Cover and leave to steam for 20 minutes.

7. Remove the lid and leave the rice to stand for about 5 minutes before fluffing it with a fork to serve.

INGREDIENT TIP: If you prefer hardier vegetables—such as carrots, potatoes, or winter squash—add them raw with the water, letting them cook with the rice. Any delicate raw vegetables, or frozen and defrosted veggies, should be added at the end and left to steam to get the best flavor and to avoid mushiness.

South Indian-Style Mushroom Pilau

Khumb Pilau

Ⓥ VEGAN | SERVES 6

PREP TIME: 15 TO 20 MINUTES | COOK TIME: 4 HOURS ON LOW OR 2 HOURS ON HIGH

This is a South Indian–style recipe that was given to me by an amazing head chef I worked with. He was from Kerala, a southwestern-coast state, and he knew a thing or two about Indian food. The flavors are incredible, and it's lovely to incorporate some traditional South Indian flavors from curry leaves, anise, and black pepper. I would urge you to try this with morel mushrooms, because their earthy flavor works wonderfully with the dish, but any combination of mushrooms will taste great.

2 cups basmati rice

2 to 3 tablespoons rapeseed oil

2 teaspoons cumin seeds

1 teaspoon fennel seeds

2 cloves

2 bay leaves

2¾-inch (7-cm) piece cassia bark

3 green cardamom pods

2 whole star anise

2 blades mace, or ½ teaspoon ground

20 curry leaves

2 onions, finely chopped

2¾-inch (7-cm) piece fresh ginger, crushed in a mortar and pestle

6 garlic cloves, crushed in a mortar and pestle

2 fresh green chiles, finely chopped

2 tomatoes, finely chopped

2 teaspoons coriander seeds, ground

1 teaspoon turmeric

1 teaspoon Garam Masala (page 23)

1 to 2 teaspoons red chili powder

½ teaspoon freshly ground black pepper

1 teaspoon salt

10 ounces (300 g) morel, or other mushrooms, cut into chunks

Handful mint leaves, chopped

Handful fresh coriander leaves, chopped

2½ cups (600 mL) hot water

1. Rinse the rice in running water until the water runs clear. Soak the rice for 10 minutes in enough water to cover it, then drain and set aside.

2. Heat the oil in a frying pan (or in the slow cooker if you have a sear setting). Add the cumin seeds, fennel seeds, cloves, bay leaves, cassia bark, green cardamom pods, anise, and mace. Stir in the curry leaves, and when fragrant, add the chopped onions and sauté until they are translucent, about 5 minutes.

3. Add the ginger, garlic, and green chiles and cook for 2 minutes.

4. Add the chopped tomatoes and sauté for another few minutes.

5. Stir in the ground coriander seeds, turmeric, garam masala powder, red chili powder, black pepper, and salt.

6. Pour everything into the slow cooker. Add the mushrooms, mint, and coriander leaves, then add the hot water and stir.

7. Add the rice and season again with salt.

8. Cover and cook on high for 2 hours or on low for 4 hours. Stir a couple of times during cooking.

9. The water should all be absorbed. Remove the lid and allow the rice to sit for 5 minutes.

10. Fluff with a fork and serve.

- -

TECHNIQUE TIP: If you feel that your rice isn't soft enough, add a little more water during the cooking time.

Fragrant Chicken Biryani

Lucknow Murgh Biryani

 CONTAINS NUTS | SERVES 6 TO 8

PREP TIME: 35 MINUTES | COOK TIME: 6 HOURS ON LOW OR 3 TO 4 HOURS ON HIGH

Biryani is an explosion of aromatics and flavors that delivers a beautiful balance of texture, spice, and heat in every bite. This is a Lucknow-style, or "pukka," biryani, meaning that the meat is cooked first in a masala before layering and baking it. I am not shy about using whole spices like peppercorns and green cardamom pods, which are necessary for creating the different layers of flavors. The nuts and texture of the rice all play a part in making this a royal dish. Saffron is traditionally used in a biryani, but don't feel pressured to spend the small fortune needed to add it. You can just leave it (and the milk) out.

FOR THE MARINADE

1 cup Greek yogurt

1 tablespoon Kashmiri chili powder

1 teaspoon salt

1 teaspoon chili powder

1 teaspoon Garam Masala (page 23)

1 teaspoon cumin seeds, ground

1 teaspoon freshly grated ginger

½ teaspoon turmeric

1 garlic clove, thinly sliced

FOR THE MASALA

4 tablespoons ghee

3 medium onions, cut into rings

1 teaspoon freshly grated ginger

2 garlic cloves, sliced

2 bay leaves

2¾-inch (7-cm) piece cassia bark

1 teaspoon black peppercorns

1 teaspoon coriander seeds

1 teaspoon cumin seeds

2 black cardamom pods (optional)

6 green cardamom pods

5 cloves

½ teaspoon salt

1 teaspoon turmeric

2 tomatoes, each cut into 8 pieces

Handful mint leaves with stems, chopped

Handful fresh coriander leaves with stems, chopped

2 or 3 fresh green chiles

4 to 6 chicken thigh fillets, chopped into chunks, or 4 to 6 legs and thighs, skinned and trimmed

FOR THE BIRYANI

1 teaspoon saffron

5 tablespoons milk

2 cups basmati rice

1 tablespoon pandan water

1 teaspoon salt

3 teaspoons ghee, divided

¼ cup fresh coriander leaves, chopped

¼ cup fresh mint leaves, chopped

Handful roasted cashew nuts

TO MAKE THE MARINADE

1. Mix all the marinade ingredients together in a bowl.

2. Add the chicken to the marinade. Stir all the flavors into the chicken and set aside for a minimum of 10 minutes (or longer).

TO MAKE THE MASALA

1. In a large sauté pan, heat the ghee and add the sliced onion rings. Cook over medium heat until they are caramelized and are a lovely dark golden-brown color, about 10 minutes. Remove half of the cooked onions and set aside.

2. To the remaining onions, add the ginger, garlic, bay leaves, cassia bark, black peppercorns, coriander seeds, cumin seeds, black and green cardamom pods, cloves, salt, and turmeric. Cook for 1 minute, until fragrant.

3. Add the tomatoes to the pan with the mint, coriander leaves, and chiles. Add the marinated chicken, stirring and cooking for a few minutes, then set aside.

TO MAKE THE BIRYANI

1. In a small bowl, add the saffron to the milk. Set aside to steep.

2. Wash the rice in 3 to 4 changes of water until the water runs clear.

3. Put 4 cups (1 liter) of water in a medium pot and bring it to a boil. Add the salt, then the drained rice. Cook the rice for 6 to 7 minutes, then strain and rinse it in cold water. Spread on a tray to cool down.

4. Heat the slow cooker to high and add 1 tablespoon of ghee.

5. Spread one-third of the rice in the bottom of the slow cooker. Sprinkle with one-third of the saffron milk, one-third of the coriander leaves, one-third of the mint, one-third of the reserved onions, and half of the cashews. Spoon half of the chicken mixture on top, and dot with 1 teaspoon of ghee.

6. Layer another one-third of the rice on top, and sprinkle again with one-third each of the saffron milk, coriander leaves, mint, and onions, and half the cashews. Spoon on the remaining chicken mixture and dot with 1 teaspoon of ghee.

Continued

7. Top with all the remaining rice and sprinkle on the rest of the saffron milk, coriander leaves, mint, and caramelized onions, and add the pandan water.

8. Cover and cook on low for 6 hours, or 3 to 4 hours on high.

9. Uncover and leave the biryani to stand for a few minutes before serving.

TECHNIQUE TIP: I've given you a quick method for caramelizing the onions, but if you are really strapped for time, you can also buy precooked onions.

Spiced Lamb Biryani

Kucha Gosht Biryani

 CONTAINS NUTS | **SERVES 6 TO 8**

PREP TIME: 35 MINUTES | **COOK TIME: 6 HOURS ON LOW OR 3 TO 4 HOURS ON HIGH**

Biryani is my go-to dish whenever I eat at a restaurant; it's the dish by which I judge a restaurant—and ultimately, the chef in the kitchen. This is a difficult dish to get right, especially in a commercial kitchen, because you can't cook a large batch of it in one go and reheat it to serve; made correctly, biryani has to be cooked in individual portions—a tricky maneuver when dealing with restaurant volumes. But the slow cooker essentially works in the same way as a handi (an Indian earthenware pot). It cooks gently, allowing the delicate fragrances of all the spices to penetrate each and every grain of rice. This is very much a Hyderabad-style biryani, cooked using raw "kucha" marinated lamb. It's a wonderful dish for entertaining, because everything is in one pot. To save time, marinate the meat in the refrigerator overnight.

FOR THE MARINADE

5 tablespoons Greek yogurt

3 tablespoons ghee

1 tablespoon Kashmiri chili powder

1 tablespoon lemon juice

1 teaspoon gram flour

1 teaspoon Garam Masala (page 23)

1 teaspoon crushed fresh ginger

1 teaspoon crushed garlic

1 teaspoon salt

½ teaspoon turmeric

3 fresh green chiles, sliced lengthwise

1-inch (2½-cm) piece fresh ginger, thinly sliced

Handful fresh mint leaves, chopped

1⅓ pounds (600 g) leg of lamb, diced

FOR THE BOUQUET GARNI
(SPICES IN A TIED MUSLIN BAG)

1 teaspoon fennel seeds

1 teaspoon coriander seeds

1 teaspoon cumin seeds

10 black peppercorns

6 cloves

5 green cardamom pods

3 black cardamom pods

1 blade mace

1 whole star anise

2¾-inch (7-cm) piece cassia bark

FOR THE BIRYANI

2 cups basmati rice

1 pinch saffron (optional)

3 tablespoons milk (optional)

2 tablespoons ghee, divided

2 onions, cut into rings

4 cups (1 liter) water

½ teaspoon cumin seeds

½ teaspoon salt

Handful mint leaves, chopped

Handful fresh coriander leaves, chopped

½ teaspoon cardamom powder

½ teaspoon Garam Masala (page 23)

Handful cashew nuts, toasted

1 tablespoon pandan water

1 teaspoon rose water (optional)

Continued

TO MAKE THE MARINADE

1. Mix all of the marinade ingredients together in a bowl.

2. Add the meat to the marinade. Stir all the flavors into the meat and set aside for 20 to 30 minutes while you prepare everything else.

TO MAKE THE BOUQUET GARNI

1. Combine all of the ingredients in a small square of muslin cloth.

2. Tie up the square with a piece of kitchen twine, so you have a little bag.

TO MAKE THE BIRYANI

1. Wash the rice in several changes of water, until the water runs clear. Set the rice aside to soak in warm water for 30 minutes.

2. In a small bowl, add the saffron to the milk (if using). Set aside to steep.

3. Heat the 1 tablespoon of ghee in a frying pan and add the onion slices. Sauté until dark brown, 8 to 10 minutes, remove, and place on some paper towels.

4. Place the bouquet garni into a pot, add the water, and bring to a boil. Simmer for 5 minutes so the water becomes fragrant.

5. Bring the water back to a boil and remove the bouquet garni. Add the cumin seeds, salt, and drained rice. Simmer for 6 to 7 minutes, until the rice is almost cooked but has a slight bite to it.

6. Drain the rice, saving 1 cup of the fragrant water. Rinse the rice in cold water and leave to cool.

7. Heat the slow cooker to either sear or high. Put 1 tablespoon of ghee in the bottom. Add the marinated lamb, and cook it for 3 to 4 minutes. Reduce the heat to low and sprinkle half of the rice over the lamb, along with 1 tablespoon of the fragranced rice water.

8. Over the layer of rice, sprinkle half of the chopped mint, half of the coriander leaves, half of the crispy onions, ¼ teaspoon of the cardamom powder, ¼ teaspoon of the garam masala, and all of the toasted cashew nuts.

9. Top with the rest of the rice, then add the remaining mint, coriander leaves, cooked onions, cardamom powder, and garam masala.

10. Sprinkle with the rest of the saffron milk, pandan water, and rose water (if using) over the top, and dot with the remaining ghee around the edges of the rice.

11. Cover the cooker and cook on low for 6 hours, or on high for 3 to 4 hours.

12. Remove the lid, and leave the dish to rest for 5 minutes before serving.

SERVING TIP: Since this is a dry dish, you'll want to pair it with a raita, which is the traditional way to serve this meal. I love it with a Pomegranate Raita (page 172) or a Red Lentil Dhal (page 70)!

Red Lentil Dhal *page 70*

Chapter Five

Dhal

Lentils and Beans

Red Lentil Dhal

Masoor di Dhal

⚛ QUICK PREP ◔ VEGETARIAN | SERVES 6

PREP TIME: 10 MINUTES | COOK TIME: 4 HOURS ON LOW OR 2 HOURS ON HIGH

This is the first dhal I learned to cook. It's simple, fresh, delicious, and a perfect meal for breakfast, lunch, or dinner. As I mentioned in chapter 2, tharka is a kind of fragrant oil, made by tempering whole spices such as cumin, mustard seed, or garlic in hot oil or ghee to intensify their natural flavors. It's added either at the beginning of the cooking process, serving as the dish's base flavor or, more commonly with dhals, at the end.

2 cups red lentils (masoor)

1 small onion, chopped

1 teaspoon salt

1 bay leaf

3 garlic cloves, chopped

2 tomatoes, finely chopped

1 teaspoon freshly grated ginger

1 teaspoon turmeric

1 or 2 fresh green chiles, finely chopped

4 cups (1 liter) hot water

1 tablespoon ghee or vegetable oil

1 teaspoon cumin seeds

1 dried red chile

1 teaspoon dried fenugreek leaves

1 teaspoon Garam Masala (page 23)

Chopped fresh coriander leaves, for garnish

1. Preheat the slow cooker on high.

2. Clean and wash the lentils.

3. Place the lentils, onion, salt, bay leaf, garlic, tomatoes, ginger, turmeric, chiles, and hot water into the slow cooker. Cover and cook on high for 2 hours, or on low for 4 hours.

4. Make the tharka to finish the dish: Heat the ghee or vegetable oil in a frying pan and add the cumin seeds. Cook until fragrant, about 1 minute. Then add the whole dried chile. Toast for a second, then pour into the cooked lentils. Stir in the fenugreek and garam masala.

5. Check the seasoning, and if required, add a little salt. Top with a pinch of coriander leaves to serve. If you prefer your dhal a little thicker, leave it to simmer with the lid off until it has thickened.

- -

TECHNIQUE TIP: When making the tharka, tilt the pan so you get a pool of oil. Then add the spices to the oil pool. Cook until you can smell the wonderful aroma.

Black Lentil Dhal

Dhal Makhani

 QUICK PREP   VEGETARIAN | SERVES 6

PREP TIME: 10 MINUTES | COOK TIME: 10 HOURS ON LOW OR 8 HOURS ON HIGH

Simple food at its best, this beautiful old-style dhal is poor man's fodder—rich in protein thanks to the black lentils (urid beans). Traditionally, the dish would be cooked gently for hours over the glowing embers of a dying fire, creating a thick, buttery consistency. This style of slow cooking isn't always possible in the Western world, which is why the slow cooker is a perfect way to achieve those authentic flavors. A great dish to cook overnight.

2 cups dry whole black lentils (urid dhal)

1 medium onion, finely chopped

1 heaped tablespoon freshly grated ginger

3 garlic cloves, chopped

3 fresh tomatoes, puréed, or 7 to 8 ounces (200 g) canned tomatoes, blended

2 fresh green chiles, chopped

2 tablespoons ghee

½ teaspoon turmeric

1 teaspoon chili powder

2 teaspoons coriander seeds, ground

1 teaspoon cumin seeds, ground

1 teaspoon sea salt

6⅓ cups (1½ liters) water

1 to 2 tablespoons butter (optional)

1 teaspoon Garam Masala (page 23)

1 teaspoon dried fenugreek leaves (kasoori methi)

Handful fresh coriander leaves, chopped

1. Preheat the slow cooker on high.

2. Clean and wash the black lentils.

3. Put the lentils, onion, ginger, garlic, tomatoes, chiles, ghee, turmeric, chili powder, coriander seeds, cumin seeds, salt, and water into the slow cooker. Cover and cook for 10 hours on low or for 8 hours on high.

4. When the lentils are cooked and creamy, stir in the butter (if using), garam masala, and fenugreek leaves to make the dhal rich and delicious. Garnish with a sprinkle of fresh coriander leaves and serve.

INGREDIENT TIP: Dried fenugreek leaves (kasoori methi, or qasuri) are one of my key ingredients, especially for North Indian and Punjabi dishes. The dried herb or powder adds an amazing earthiness and a delicious aroma. It's a little more difficult to come by, but if you have a local Indian store they will stock it. If not, order it online.

Earthy Whole Brown Lentil Dhal

Sabat Masoor di Dhal

⊛ QUICK PREP　◔ VEGETARIAN | SERVES 6

PREP TIME: 10 MINUTES | COOK TIME: 8 HOURS ON LOW OR 6 HOURS ON HIGH

I have vivid recollections of my mum cooking this dish using the ominous pressure cooker. The feeling of terror when that contraption hissed and then released its pressure still fills me with dread. But the negative feeling quickly dissipates when I remember the aromas released by this whole brown dhal, with a swirl of melting butter in the middle of the bowl and a puffed-up roti in my hand ready for dipping! I find the slow cooker a much gentler way to cook than the pressure cooker—no scary hissing involved.

6⅓ cups (1½ liters) hot water

2 cups whole brown lentils (sabut masoor)

1 tablespoon ghee

1 teaspoon freshly grated ginger

1 teaspoon sea salt

1 teaspoon turmeric

7 to 8 ounces (200 g) canned tomatoes

4 garlic cloves, finely chopped

1 or 2 fresh green chiles, finely chopped

1 onion, chopped

1 teaspoon Garam Masala (page 23)

Handful fresh coriander leaves, chopped

1. Wash and clean the lentils, then set them aside to drain.

2. Heat the slow cooker to high and add all of the ingredients except the garam masala and coriander leaves.

3. Cover and cook on high for 6 hours, or on low for 8 hours.

4. Add the garam masala and fresh coriander leaves before serving, and enjoy.

INGREDIENT TIP: Whole lentils will take longer to cook than split ones, and some will require soaking overnight—except when you cook them in a slow cooker.

Dry-Cooked Yellow Mung Beans

Sooke Moong Dhal

✳ QUICK PREP ⓥ VEGAN | SERVES 6

PREP TIME: 10 MINUTES | COOK TIME: 2 HOURS ON LOW OR 1 HOUR ON HIGH

Although the dhals you get in Indian restaurants tend to be more like a stew or a thick soup, moong dhal can also be cooked so that its consistency is somewhat dry. When prepared this way, the dhal takes on a nutty flavor. Don't skip the lime at the end, as the citrus adds a delicious, tangy burst.

2 cups yellow mung beans (moong dhal)

2-inch (5-cm) piece fresh ginger, roughly chopped

2 fresh green chiles

1 tablespoon rapeseed oil

1 teaspoon mustard seeds

1 teaspoon cumin seeds

2 dried red chiles

1 bay leaf

1 teaspoon chili powder

1 teaspoon turmeric

1 teaspoon coriander seeds, ground

1 teaspoon salt

⅓ cup (100 mL) water

1 lime, quartered

1. Wash the mung beans in several changes of water, until the water runs clear. Drain the beans and leave them in the sieve.

2. In a mortar and pestle, pound the ginger with the green chiles to form a paste.

3. Heat the oil in a frying pan (or in the slow cooker if you have a sear setting). Add the mustard and cumin seeds. When they begin to crackle, add the dried red chiles, the bay leaf, and the ginger-and-green-chile paste. Cook for a few seconds.

4. Transfer everything to the slow cooker. Add the yellow mung beans and mix.

5. Add the chili powder, turmeric, coriander seeds, salt, and water, then stir.

6. Cover and cook on low for 2 hours, or on high for 1 hour.

7. Check the dhal is cooked by squeezing a bit between your fingers; if it's soft, the dhal is ready. If it's still fairly wet you can turn the cooker to high and reduce the excess liquid until you are happy with the consistency. A good squeeze of lime just before serving makes this dish super tasty.

Black Lentils with Split Chickpeas

Mahaar Chole di Dhal

QUICK PREP | **VEGAN** | SERVES 6

PREP TIME: 10 MINUTES | **COOK TIME: 10 HOURS ON LOW OR 8 HOURS ON HIGH**

Another North Indian classic, this dhal is made with split chickpeas and black lentils. It's always served at Sikh temples as part of the langar, or community kitchen. As a child, my mum would always cook this with very few chiles, so it was nice and mild for the children to have with rice and some butter. Being so wholesome and nutritious, the food was good for growing children. When cooked gently, the lentils break down just enough to produce a thick, rich gravy, so using a slow cooker works perfectly.

4 cups (1 liter) water

¾ cup split gram (channa dhal), washed

¾ cup black lentils (urid beans), washed and checked for stones

7 to 8 ounces (200 g) canned tomatoes

1 tablespoon vegetable oil

1 heaped teaspoon freshly grated ginger

1 teaspoon turmeric

1 teaspoon salt

2 garlic cloves, minced

2 fresh green chiles, finely chopped

1 onion, finely diced

1 teaspoon Garam Masala (page 23)

Handful fresh coriander leaves, chopped

1. Preheat the slow cooker on high.

2. Add all of the ingredients except the garam masala and coriander leaves, and cook on low for 10 hours, or on high for 8 hours.

3. To serve, sprinkle with garam masala and coriander leaves.

Garlicky Split Chickpea Curry

Channa Dhal

⊛ **QUICK PREP** Ⓥ **VEGAN** | **SERVES 6**

PREP TIME: 10 MINUTES | **COOK TIME: 6 HOURS ON LOW OR 4 HOURS ON HIGH**

This wholesome dhal is made with split black chickpeas whose skin has been removed. The dhal has a sweet, nutty flavor and is finished with a garlic tharka, giving it an amazing boost. This recipe is very much a North Indian way of cooking this dhal. If you can't get channa, you can also make this dish with split pigeon peas (toor dhal) or split yellow peas (yellow moong). Served with Plain Basmati Rice (page 180), the dish makes a hearty midweek dinner.

1½ cups split gram (channa dhal)

1 onion, finely chopped

2 tomatoes, chopped

1 tablespoon freshly grated ginger

1 teaspoon cumin seeds, ground or crushed with a mortar and pestle

2 teaspoons turmeric

2 garlic cloves, crushed

1 hot green Thai or other fresh chile, thinly sliced

3 cups (750 mL) hot water

1 teaspoon salt

2 tablespoons rapeseed oil

1 teaspoon cumin seeds, crushed

1 garlic clove, sliced

1 fresh green chile, sliced

1. Heat the slow cooker to high. Add the split gram, onion, tomatoes, ginger, crushed cumin seeds, turmeric, crushed garlic, hot chile, water, and salt, and then stir.

2. Cover and cook on high for 4 hours, or on low for 6 hours, until the split gram is tender.

3. Just before serving, heat the oil in a saucepan. When the oil is hot, add the cumin seeds with the sliced garlic. Cook until the garlic is golden brown, and then pour it over the dhal.

4. To serve, top with the sliced green chile.

SERVING TIP: For a little freshness, add a handful of coriander leaves just before serving.

Chickpea Curry

Channa Masala

⊛ QUICK PREP Ⓥ VEGAN | SERVES 6

PREP TIME: 10 MINUTES | COOK TIME: 10 HOURS ON LOW OR 8 HOURS ON HIGH

Chickpeas are known by various names in India, such as channa and chole. This amazing, flavorful legume can be used and cooked in many different ways, including the ever-popular channa masala. It is best cooked slowly, so the chickpeas cook through and absorb the flavor of the masala—yet another dish perfect for the slow cooker. I love to serve the curry with some fried poori (a puffy flatbread).

2 cups dried chickpeas (channa)

1 tablespoon rapeseed oil

2 teaspoons cumin seeds

2 bay leaves

2¾-inch (7-cm) piece cassia bark

2 medium onions, thinly sliced

1 teaspoon salt

1 tablespoon freshly grated ginger

6 garlic cloves, finely chopped

2 fresh green chiles, chopped

2 medium tomatoes, finely chopped

1 teaspoon Kashmiri chili powder

2 teaspoons coriander seeds, ground

½ teaspoon turmeric

2 teaspoons mango powder

½ teaspoon black salt

4 cups (1 liter) hot water

1 tablespoon lemon juice

Sliced red onions, for garnish

Fresh coriander leaves, roughly chopped, for garnish

2 fresh green chiles sliced lengthwise

1 teaspoon Chaat Masala (page 23)

1. Wash the chickpeas and set them aside to drain.

2. Heat the oil in a frying pan (or in the slow cooker if you have a sear setting). Add the cumin seeds, bay leaves, and cassia bark, and cook until fragrant, about 1 minute.

3. Stir in the sliced onions and salt, and cook for 5 to 6 minutes. Add the ginger, garlic, and chopped chiles and stir for 1 to 2 minutes.

4. Transfer to the slow cooker. Then add the chickpeas, tomatoes, chili powder, ground coriander seeds, turmeric, mango powder, black salt, and hot water.

5. Cover and cook for 10 hours on low, or for 8 hours on high.

6. Leave the cooker on warm until ready to serve. Then top with sliced red onions, freshly chopped coriander leaves, sliced green chiles, and a sprinkle of chaat masala.

SIMPLE SUBSTITUTION: If you don't have the mango powder (amchoor), use a squeeze of fresh lime to get that tangy brightness into the dish, which is so important. If you don't have black salt, a bit more mango powder, chaat masala, or a squeeze of lemon will do.

Kale with Chickpeas

Channa Saag

✴ QUICK PREP Ⓥ VEGAN | SERVES 6

PREP TIME: 10 MINUTES | COOK TIME: 6 HOURS ON LOW OR 4 HOURS ON HIGH

I love this dish because it's such a favorite on my website. You would usually cook it with spinach, but in this recipe I have swapped it for kale, as this hardy cabbage has more flavor and greater nutritional value. The texture works so beautifully with the bite of the spicy chickpeas. Serve with poori and some fresh plain yogurt.

1 to 2 tablespoons rapeseed oil

½ teaspoon mustard seeds

1 teaspoon cumin seeds

1 large onion, diced

4 garlic cloves, crushed

4 plum tomatoes, finely chopped

1 heaped teaspoon coriander seeds, ground

1 fresh green chile, chopped

1 teaspoon chili powder

1 teaspoon turmeric

1 teaspoon salt

2 (16-ounce/450-g) cans cooked chickpeas, drained and rinsed

¾ cup (200 mL) water

7 to 8 ounces (200 g) kale, chopped

1 fresh green chile, sliced, for garnish

1. Heat the oil in a frying pan (or in the slow cooker if you have a sear setting). When it's hot add the mustard seeds and then the cumin seeds until they pop and become fragrant.

2. Add the diced onion and cook, stirring, for 10 minutes. Add the garlic and cook for a few minutes. Then add the tomatoes. Add the ground coriander seeds, green chile, chili powder, turmeric, and salt.

3. Add the chickpeas and water. Cover and cook on low for 6 hours, or on high for 4 hours.

4. Add the chopped kale, a handful at a time, stirring between. Leave this to cook for another 10 to 15 minutes, until the kale is soft and tender.

5. Top with the sliced chile.

SIMPLE SUBSTITUTION: If you can't find kale, or if you don't like it, use spinach or even cabbage.

Split Chickpeas with Turnips

Shalgum Channa Dhal

 QUICK PREP Ⓥ VEGAN | SERVES 6

PREP TIME: 10 MINUTES | COOK TIME: 6 TO 7 HOURS ON LOW OR 4 TO 5 HOURS ON HIGH

A lovely dhal cooked with turnips, whose wonderful texture is a great way to bulk out this delicious lentil dish. In a slow cooker these hardy root vegetables cook so beautifully and taste amazing. If you'd like, garnish this dish with a little butter.

2 teaspoons cumin seeds, divided

1 teaspoon mustard seeds

1 teaspoon coriander seeds

1 tablespoon rapeseed oil

1½-inch (4-cm) piece cassia bark

4 small turnips, peeled and chopped

1 cup dried split chickpeas (channa dhal), washed

4 cups (1 liter) hot water

3 ripe tomatoes, chopped finely

1 or 2 fresh green chiles, chopped

1½-inch (4-cm) piece fresh ginger, grated

1 small onion, sliced

2 garlic cloves, sliced

½ teaspoon turmeric

1 teaspoon salt

½ teaspoon chili powder

Handful fresh coriander leaves, chopped

1. Preheat the slow cooker on high.

2. Place 1 teaspoon of the cumin seeds, and the mustard, and coriander seeds in a dry frying pan and roast until they turn a shade darker and become fragrant. Crush the spices in a mortar and pestle or a spice grinder.

3. Add the oil to the slow cooker and heat. Then add the cassia bark and the remaining cumin seeds and cook for a few moments.

4. Put the turnips, split chickpeas, and water into the slow cooker. Then add the tomatoes, green chiles, ginger, onion, and garlic. Stir in the turmeric, salt, chili powder, and ground spices.

5. Cook on high for 4 hours, or on low for 6 hours. If you want to thicken the dhal, remove the lid and cook on high for another 30 minutes to 1 hour.

6. Once soft and cooked through, add the chopped coriander leaves.

- -

SIMPLE SUBSTITUTION: This dish will also work with other hearty vegetables, such as radishes or even winter squash for a slightly sweet flavor. Use whatever is fresh and available.

Black Chickpeas

Kaala Channa

⚙ QUICK PREP   Ⓥ VEGAN | SERVES 6

PREP TIME: 10 MINUTES | COOK TIME: 11 HOURS ON LOW OR 9 HOURS ON HIGH

Noticeably different from light chickpeas, black channa have a thicker skin and are more robust—and they take a lot longer to cook. But they have a tremendous warming character. A kind of a home remedy in our house, my mum will cook this if she's not feeling 100 percent, and will have a bowlful of the gravy, with roti for dipping. Whether eaten for its potential health-boosting properties or not, the meal is really tasty and nutritious.

1 tablespoon rapeseed oil

2 teaspoons cumin seeds

2 cups dried whole black chickpeas, washed

4 cups (1 liter) hot water

1 onion, roughly chopped

2-inch (5-cm) piece fresh ginger, peeled and roughly chopped

4 garlic cloves

3 fresh green chiles

1 tomato, roughly chopped

1 teaspoon turmeric

1 teaspoon Kashmiri chili powder

1 teaspoon sea salt

Handful fresh corlander leaves, chopped

Juice of 1 lemon

1. Heat the oil in a frying pan (or in the slow cooker if you have a sear setting). Add the cumin seeds until they sizzle, then pour them into the cooker.

2. Heat the slow cooker to high, and then add the chickpeas and water.

3. In a blender, purée the onion, ginger, garlic, chiles, and tomato to make a paste. Add it to the cooker, along with the turmeric, chili powder, and salt.

4. Cover and cook for 9 hours on high, or for 11 hours on low.

5. When the chickpeas are cooked, check the seasoning. Add the coriander leaves and lemon juice, and serve.

- -

TECHNIQUE TIP: For a thicker gravy, once cooked use the back of your spoon to squash the beans a little—black channa will remain firmer than other types of beans.

Punjabi Red Kidney Bean Curry

Punjabi Rajma

Ⓥ **VEGAN** | **SERVES 6**

PREP TIME: 15 MINUTES, PLUS OVERNIGHT TO SOAK THE BEANS | **COOK TIME: 8 HOURS ON LOW OR 6 HOURS ON HIGH**

This is the basic home dish of all Punjabi families, served with fresh and fragrant basmati rice—a delicious and super-nutritious meal. This kind of plain home cooking is not usually served in restaurants or even at takeout places, but it's eaten in Punjabi homes almost daily. Think of it as an Indian chili—robust and nutritious.

1½ cups red kidney beans, soaked overnight

4 cups (1 liter) hot water

7 to 8 ounces (200 g) canned plum tomatoes

2 teaspoons freshly grated ginger

1 teaspoon salt, plus more for seasoning

1 teaspoon turmeric

4 garlic cloves, finely chopped

1 or 2 fresh green chiles, sliced

1 onion, finely diced

1 teaspoon Garam Masala (page 23)

Handful fresh coriander leaves, chopped

1 teaspoon butter (optional)

1. Soak the kidney beans overnight, then rinse. If you have a boil function on your slow cooker, cover the beans with water and boil for 10 minutes. If not, do this in a large pot. Drain and put the beans back into the slow cooker.

2. Add all the ingredients except the garam masala, coriander leaves, and butter. Add the water and cook on low for 8 hours, or on high for 6 hours.

3. Add the garam masala, chopped coriander leaves, and butter (if using). Season with salt and serve.

INGREDIENT TIP: Always boil your kidney beans for 10 minutes before cooking, to make sure they are thoroughly cleared of their natural toxins (see tip on page 28).

South Indian Split Yellow Pigeon Peas with Mixed Vegetables

Sambar

 VEGAN | SERVES 6

PREP TIME: 20 MINUTES | **COOK TIME: 6½ HOURS ON LOW OR 4½ HOURS ON HIGH**

Sambar is a classic South Indian dish of pigeon peas and vegetables, and a necessity when you have a traditional thali (a meal from the South consisting of rice and six or seven other dishes—think Indian tapas—served on banana leaves). You start with the sambar masala, a flavor base, and then add the dhal and vegetables. It's eaten with steamed rice cakes known as idlis, or with lentil crepes called dosa—the combination is amazing.

FOR THE SAMBAR MASALA

1 teaspoon rapeseed oil

3 tablespoons coriander seeds

2 tablespoons split gram (channa dhal)

1 teaspoon black peppercorns

½ teaspoon fenugreek seeds

½ teaspoon mustard seeds

¼ teaspoon cumin seeds

12 whole dried red chiles

FOR THE SAMBAR

1½ cups split yellow pigeon peas (toor dhal), washed

2 fresh green chiles, sliced lengthwise

2 garlic cloves, chopped

6 pearl onions

4 to 5 tablespoons sambar masala

2 teaspoons salt

1 to 2 carrots, peeled and chopped

1 red potato, peeled and diced

1 white radish (mooli), peeled and chopped into 2¾-inch (7-cm) sticks

1 tomato, roughly chopped

4 cups (1 liter) water

2 to 3 moringa seed pods, or ⅓ pound (150 g) green beans or asparagus, chopped into 2¾-inch (7-cm) lengths

2 tablespoons tamarind paste

½ teaspoon asafetida

2 teaspoons coconut oil

1 teaspoon mustard seeds

20 curry leaves

2 dried red chilies

Handful fresh coriander leaves, chopped (optional)

TO MAKE THE SAMBAR MASALA

1. Add the oil to a medium nonstick skillet. Add all of the remaining ingredients and roast for a few minutes until fragrant. The spices will brown a little, but don't let them burn.

2. Remove from the heat and pour onto a plate to cool. Once cooled, place into your spice grinder or mortar and pestle and grind to a powder. Set aside.

TO MAKE THE SAMBAR

1. Heat the slow cooker to high and add the pigeon peas, green chiles, garlic, pearl onions, sambar masala, salt, carrots, potatoes, radish, tomato, and water.

2. Cover and cook for 4 hours on high, or for 6 hours on low.

3. Add the moringa (or green beans or asparagus), tamarind paste, and asafetida. Cover and cook for another 30 minutes.

4. When you're ready to serve, heat the coconut oil in a frying pan and pop the mustard seeds with the curry leaves and dried chiles. Pour over the sambar. Top with coriander leaves (if using) and serve.

INGREDIENT TIP: Moringa seed pods (called drumsticks) are a bit of an Indian superfood. They are long beanlike veggies that come from the moringa tree (also known as the horseradish tree), and are used in many curries across South India. The bark, root, sap, flowers, and seeds are used in traditional medicine and are thought to have cold-fighting properties. The seed pods and leaves are high in iron and vitamin C, and are often given to children and pregnant women. Drumsticks are traditional in sambar, especially in Tamil Nadu and Kerala. They add a very delicate fragrance. But if you can't find this vegetable, substitute green beans or asparagus.

Spiced Chickpeas and Potatoes *page 88*

Chapter Six

Vegetables

Potatoes with Cumin

Jeera Aloo

⊛ QUICK PREP Ⓥ VEGAN | SERVES 6

PREP TIME: 10 MINUTES | COOK TIME: 4 HOURS ON LOW OR 2 TO 3 HOURS ON HIGH

A bit different from the usual Bombay potatoes, this fabulous side dish of cumin-fragranced potatoes is characteristically earthy. And the amchoor gives it a delightful zing. I like to serve this kind of simple potato dish with plain paratha (a flatbread) for brunch or as a side to a rich lamb curry. You can also cook this with small baby potatoes—just scrub and leave the potatoes whole and prick them with a sharp knife to help the flavors penetrate.

2 teaspoons cumin seeds, divided

1 tablespoon coriander seeds

2 tablespoons vegetable oil

1 onion, sliced

2 fresh green chiles, sliced lengthwise

1-inch (3-cm) piece fresh ginger, sliced very thinly

¼ teaspoon turmeric

1 teaspoon chili powder

Sea salt

6 large potatoes, peeled and chopped into 1½-inch (4-cm) chunks

½ cup (100 mL) hot water

2 teaspoons mango powder (amchoor), or a squeeze of lemon juice

Handful fresh coriander leaves, chopped

1. Preheat the slow cooker on high.

2. Meanwhile, in a dry frying pan toast 1 teaspoon of the cumin seeds along with all of the coriander seeds. Once fragrant, remove from the heat and crush in a mortar and pestle or spice grinder.

3. To the hot slow cooker, add the oil, onion, sliced green chiles, ginger, and remaining 1 teaspoon of cumin seeds. Stir, and then add the roasted spice powder, turmeric, chili powder, and salt.

4. Add the cubed potatoes and mix well. Then add the water. Cover and cook on high for 2 to 3 hours, or on low for 4 hours.

5. Stir in the mango powder and garnish with coriander leaves to serve.

Potato and Eggplant Curry

Aloo Bangun

QUICK PREP | **VEGAN** | SERVES 6

PREP TIME: 10 MINUTES | COOK TIME: 3 TO 4 HOURS ON LOW OR 2 HOURS ON HIGH

I can't even describe how delicious this classic North Indian dish of eggplant and potatoes really is. Because eggplant is naturally warming, I never use garlic with it—just doesn't need it. When using a slow cooker, season the dish with salt when you are about to serve, because if you add the salt before cooking it will draw out too much liquid from the vegetables.

2 tablespoons mustard oil

2 teaspoons mustard seeds

2 teaspoons cumin seeds

1 onion, finely sliced

7 to 8 ounces (200 g) canned tomatoes

1 teaspoon turmeric

1 fresh green chile, finely chopped

1 tablespoon freshly grated ginger

2 eggplants, about 1 pound (500 g) total, cut into 1-inch (3-cm) lengths

2 red potatoes, peeled and cut into 1-inch (3-cm) lengths

1 teaspoon sea salt

1 teaspoon Garam Masala (page 23)

Handful fresh coriander leaves, chopped

1. Heat the oil in a frying pan (or in the slow cooker if you have a sear setting). Add the mustard seeds, and as they are sizzling add the cumin seeds until they become fragrant.

2. Turn the slow cooker to high and add the spices with the sliced onion, tomatoes, turmeric, chopped chile, and grated ginger.

3. Stir in the eggplant and potatoes. Cover and cook on high for 2 hours, or for 3 to 4 hours on low.

4. When you are ready to serve, add the salt, garam masala, and fresh coriander leaves.

INGREDIENT TIP: Depending on the eggplants you use, they may contain a lot of water (large Italian ones tend to be more moist)—meaning you may have to cook the dish in the slow cooker with the lid off for an additional hour or so. Adding the salt at the end of cooking will help.

Spiced Chickpeas and Potatoes
Aloo Chole

 VEGAN | **SERVES 6**

PREP TIME: 15 MINUTES | **COOK TIME: 10 HOURS ON LOW OR 8 HOURS ON HIGH**

Chickpeas and potatoes are a delicious classic combination that works so amazingly with this robust masala. I love to add a citrus twist to the final dish, making it light and fragrant. This side pairs deliciously with poori.

1 tablespoon rapeseed oil

2 teaspoons cumin seeds

2 bay leaves

2 ¾-inch (7-cm) piece cassia bark

2 medium onions, thinly sliced

1 teaspoon salt

1 tablespoon freshly grated ginger

6 garlic cloves, finely chopped

2 fresh green chiles, chopped

2 cups dried chickpeas, washed

2 red potatoes, peeled and diced

2 medium tomatoes, finely chopped

1 teaspoon Kashmiri chili powder

2 teaspoons coriander seeds, ground

½ teaspoon turmeric

4 cups (1 liter) hot water

1 tablespoon fresh lemon juice

Fresh coriander leaves, roughly chopped, for garnish

1 teaspoon Chaat Masala (page 23)

2 fresh green chiles, sliced lengthwise

1. Heat the oil in a frying pan (or in the slow cooker if you have a sear setting). Add the cumin seeds, bay leaves, and cassia bark, and cook until fragrant, about 1 minute.

2. Stir in the sliced onions and salt, and cook for 5 to 6 minutes. Add the ginger, garlic, and chopped chiles, and tir for 1 to 2 minutes.

3. Pour the mixture into the slow cooker with the chickpeas, potatoes, tomatoes, chili powder, coriander seeds, turmeric, and hot water.

4. Cover and cook for 10 hours on low, or for 8 hours on high. Leave on warm until ready to serve.

5. Just before serving, sprinkle with the lemon juice, chopped coriander leaves, chaat masala, and sliced green chilies.

- -

INGREDIENT TIP: If you want, use a can of cooked chickpeas. Just drain and rinse them first. And reduce the cooking time to 3 hours on high, or 4 hours on low.

Spiced Potatoes and Cauliflower

Aloo Gobi

⊛ QUICK PREP Ⓥ VEGAN | SERVES 6
PREP TIME: 10 MINUTES | COOK TIME: 3 HOURS ON LOW OR 2 HOURS ON HIGH

Aloo gobi is a traditional Punjabi dish that is a must in your Indian food repertoire—it's flavorful and is a lovely way to use cauliflower. Because it's a dry dish, it's usually cooked in a karahi (an Indian wok), and the resulting masala clings to the cauliflower florets. Amazingly, the slow cooker achieves a similarly great result, every time. Don't add any water; the cauliflower has enough liquid in it to make this dish perfect and delicious.

1 large cauliflower, cored and cut into florets

2 tablespoons mustard oil

2 teaspoons mustard seeds

2 teaspoons cumin seeds

1 onion, finely chopped

3 garlic cloves, finely chopped

2 red potatoes, peeled and cut into 1½-inch (4-cm) cubes

7 to 8 ounces (200 g) canned tomatoes

1 tablespoon freshly grated ginger

1 teaspoon salt

1 teaspoon turmeric

1 teaspoon chili powder

1 or 2 fresh green chiles, finely chopped

1 teaspoon dried fenugreek leaves

1 teaspoon Garam Masala (page 23)

Handful fresh coriander leaves, chopped

1. Prepare your cauliflower and make sure it's thoroughly dry before cooking.

2. Heat the oil in a frying pan (or in the slow cooker if you have a sear setting). Add the mustard seeds, and as they sizzle add the cumin seeds.

3. Add the onions and garlic, and cook for 1 minute before adding the potatoes and cauliflower to the slow cooker along with the tomatoes, ginger, salt, turmeric, chili powder, chopped chiles, and dried fenugreek leaves.

4. Turn the cooker to low and cook for 3 hours, or for 2 hours on high. Give the dish a stir in the first hour, and it will release enough liquid to cook.

5. Before serving, sprinkle with garam masala and fresh coriander leaves.

- -

TECHNIQUE TIP: Sometimes there will be a lot of liquid, which is full of flavor, remaining at the bottom of the slow cooker. You can use the bhuna technique of dry frying everything in a large pan on a high heat to reduce the liquid and flavor the dish. Be careful not to break up the cauliflower and potatoes—you don't want to turn them to mush.

Whole Roasted Cauliflower with Cashew Sauce
Gobi Masallum

CONTAINS NUTS | VEGETARIAN | SERVES 6
PREP TIME: 15 MINUTES | COOK TIME: 4 TO 5 HOURS ON LOW OR 2 TO 3 HOURS ON HIGH

This is a dish I have cooked on so many occasions, and it always remains a winner. Whole roasted cauliflower is a bit of a "thing" at the moment, but it's an ingredient the people of India have been enjoying for many years. A bit under-rated in the Western world, cauliflower is so versatile—it works with lots of different spices and can be cooked in so many ways. This recipe has a rich cashew sauce, which adds a creamy mouthfeel, and serving the whole head of cauliflower adds fun to your dinner table.

1 red onion, sliced

1-inch (3-cm) piece fresh ginger, cut into strips

4 garlic cloves, sliced

2 tomatoes, roughly chopped

1 fresh green chile, chopped

5 tablespoons raw cashews, soaked in water for 2 hours and drained

1 large head cauliflower, outer leaves trimmed

2 tablespoons ghee or rapeseed oil

1 teaspoon cumin seeds

1 teaspoon coriander seeds

1 teaspoon salt

1 teaspoon Kashmiri chili powder

1 teaspoon turmeric

1 teaspoon Garam Masala (page 23)

⅔ cup (160 mL) hot water

1 tablespoon dried fenugreek leaves

Handful fresh coriander leaves, chopped

1. Preheat the slow cooker on high for 15 minutes, or use the sauté setting if you have one. Add the onions, ginger, garlic, tomatoes, and green chile. Stir and cook for 10 minutes.

2. Add the drained cashews, and place the head of cauliflower on top of everything.

3. Heat the ghee or rapeseed oil, if using, in a frying pan and toast the cumin and coriander seeds until they are fragrant. Pour them over the cauliflower head and sprinkle in the salt, chili powder, turmeric, and garam masala.

4. Add the water. Cover and cook on low for 4 to 5 hours, or on high for 2 to 3 hours.

5. When it's cooked (you can check by sticking a sharp knife through the middle), transfer the cauliflower head to a shallow ovenproof dish. Using an immersion or regular blender, blend the cooking liquid that's left in the slow cooker to make a smooth sauce. It should be like a thick batter; if it's too thick you can add a little hot water.

6. Check and adjust the salt, if required. Add the dried fenugreek leaves, and then pour the sauce over the cauliflower head. Place in the oven at 400°F (200°C) for 5 to 10 minutes to crisp up.

7. Sprinkle on some fresh coriander leaves and serve in chunky wedges.

Spinach and Paneer Cheese

Saag Paneer

⚙ QUICK PREP 🥄 VEGETARIAN | SERVES 6

PREP TIME: 10 MINUTES | COOK TIME: 4 HOURS ON LOW OR 2 TO 3 HOURS ON HIGH

Palak, or spinach, is what most often comes to mind when people think of this North Indian dish. But traditionally it's made with mustard leaves, which offer a stronger bite. It works just as well with spinach, or you can add other greens if you want to, such as kale or Swiss chard. My mum sometimes even uses a little bit of broccoli. Adding some butter makes it a perfect balance of the healthy stuff with a little bit of decadence.

2 pounds (1 kg) fresh spinach

1½-inch (4-cm) piece fresh ginger, roughly chopped

5 garlic cloves, whole

2 fresh green chiles, roughly chopped

1 onion, roughly chopped

1 teaspoon salt

½ teaspoon turmeric

4 tomatoes, finely chopped

1 to 2 tablespoons cornstarch to thicken (if required)

4 tablespoons butter

1 teaspoon cumin seeds

3 garlic cloves, minced

1 tablespoon dried fenugreek leaves

2 tablespoons rapeseed oil

12 ounces paneer, cut into cubes

1. Heat the slow cooker to high and add the spinach, ginger, garlic, chiles, onion, salt, turmeric, and tomatoes.

2. Cover and cook on high for 3 hours, or on low for 6 hours.

3. Using your immersion blender or a food processor, purée the greens to a fine, glossy consistency. The aim is to have a thick and bright-green purée. If it's a little watery you may need to reduce it on the stove to thicken, or if your slow cooker has a boil function, use it to boil off a little of the liquid. You can also thicken it up by sprinkling with some cornstarch.

4. Heat the butter in a pan and add the cumin seeds until they sizzle. Then add the minced garlic and stir until it just browns. Remove from the heat. Add the dried fenugreek leaves and pour everything into the saag that's in the slow cooker. Whisk through.

5. Fry the cubes of paneer in a little oil in the same pan, until they are golden brown. Stir into the saag. Replace the lid and let everything sit for another 10 minutes before serving.

INGREDIENT TIP: Paneer is a fresh cheese, similar to farmer cheese. You'll find a recipe for homemade paneer on page 178. If you're using store-bought paneer, you can soak it in some hot water to soften before adding it to the saag.

Vegetable Korma with Almonds

Navratan Korma

 CONTAINS NUTS ⓥ VEGAN | SERVES 6

PREP TIME: 15 MINUTES | COOK TIME: 4 TO 5 HOURS ON LOW OR 2 TO 3 HOURS ON HIGH, PLUS 1 HOUR ON HIGH

Korma comes from the Mughal Dynasty, when it was cooked for the wealthy and enjoyed a prestigious status associated with the royal courts. It's an amazing dish that champions the delicious flavor and creamy texture of almonds. While some people may think of vegan food as insubstantial and bland, vegan Indian food is hearty, complex, and delicious—especially when done in the slow cooker. The white poppy seeds (khuskhus) are used to thicken the sauce, but if you can't find them, just leave them out. Serve this dish with plain rice.

1 tablespoon vegetable oil

3 cloves

3 green cardamom pods

1-inch (3-cm) piece cassia bark

1 to 3 dried red chiles

2 onions, minced

2 garlic cloves, minced

1 tablespoon freshly grated ginger

1 teaspoon turmeric

1 tablespoon coriander seeds, ground

Sea salt

⅓ cup (100 mL) hot water

⅓ cup creamed coconut

2 heaped tablespoons ground almonds

1 teaspoon white poppy seeds, ground

1 cup cauliflower florets

1 carrot, peeled and chopped

1 red bell pepper, seeded and diced

1 cup peeled, seeded, and chopped winter squash (such as butternut or pumpkin)

½ cup frozen peas, defrosted

½ cup green beans

1 teaspoon Garam Masala (page 23)

Handful fresh coriander leaves, finely chopped

3 tablespoons slivered almonds

1 squeeze fresh lemon juice

1. Heat the oil in a frying pan (or in the slow cooker if you have a sear setting). Add the cloves, cardamom pods, cassia bark, and dried red chiles. Cook for a few minutes until fragrant. Add the minced onions and sauté gently over medium heat for about 5 to 10 minutes.

2. Set the slow cooker on high and pour the mixture inside. Add the garlic and ginger and cook for a few minutes. Then stir in the turmeric, ground coriander seeds, and salt. Pour in the hot water, creamed coconut, ground almonds, and poppy seeds, and then stir.

3. Add the cauliflower, carrot, pepper, and squash. Cover and cook on high for 2 to 3 hours, or on low for 4 to 5 hours.

4. Add the peas and green beans and cook on high for another hour.

5. When the dish is cooked, add the garam masala and stir through. Top with fresh coriander leaves, slivered almonds, and a squeeze of lemon juice for added freshness.

EASY ADJUSTMENT: For extra decadence, add a pinch of saffron steeped in milk: Steep 1 teaspoon of saffron threads in 5 tablespoons of milk for 20 minutes; sprinkle the saffron milk over the dish just before serving.

Stuffed Baby Eggplants with Pickling Spices

Kalongi Bangun

V VEGAN | SERVES 6

PREP TIME: 15 MINUTES | COOK TIME: 4 HOURS ON LOW OR 2 TO 3 HOURS ON HIGH

Eggplants are my favorite vegetable—and with these robust spices, plus the tang of the mango powder, the eggplant reaches new heights. Although they are called baby eggplants, they are in fact mature, just small and round. They are also known as Indian eggplants. Meaty and not too watery, the eggplants are perfect to cook with spices. Serve this dish hot with Plain Basmati Rice (page 180) or Whole-Wheat Flatbread (page 181).

12 baby eggplants

4 dried red chiles

2 tablespoons coriander seeds

1 teaspoon mustard seeds

1 teaspoon cumin seeds

½ teaspoon fenugreek seeds

1 teaspoon fennel seeds

1 tablespoon nigella seeds

¼ teaspoon carom seeds

½ teaspoon turmeric

1 teaspoon mango powder (amchoor)

Sea salt

3 tablespoons mustard oil

2 onions, sliced

Handful fresh coriander leaves, chopped

1. Preheat the slow cooker on high.

2. Wash the eggplants and cut lengthwise, but leave the top intact.

3. Heat a dry frying pan on medium-high and add the red chiles, coriander seeds, mustard seeds, cumin seeds, fenugreek seeds, fennel seeds, nigella seeds, and carom seeds to the pan. Toast until fragrant, about 1 minute. Remove and put into a coffee grinder and blend to a fine powder.

4. Empty into a medium bowl and mix in the turmeric, mango powder, and salt. Add some water to make a thick paste.

5. Rub about 1 teaspoon of the paste into each of the eggplants with your fingers so the flesh is covered inside and out.

6. Heat the mustard oil in the same frying pan (or in the slow cooker if you have a sear setting). Add the sliced onions and cook for 5 minutes. Add any remaining spice paste. Mix for a minute or two and add a splash of water if needed. Then pour the onion mixture into the slow cooker.

7. Place the stuffed eggplants into the cooker and cover. Cook on low for 4 hours, or on high for 2 to 3 hours.

8. Turn the eggplants a few times during cooking, if possible.

9. Check the seasoning and sprinkle in the coriander leaves.

INGREDIENT TIP: Japanese eggplants are thin and long, and Italian eggplants tend to be large and oblong. If you can't find baby eggplants, use the Japanese variety, or the smallest Italian ones you can find.

Spicy Stuffed Peppers
Bharee Shimla Mirch

Ⓥ VEGAN | SERVES 4

PREP TIME: 15 MINUTES | COOK TIME: 4 HOURS ON LOW OR 2 HOURS ON HIGH

This dish reminds me of family summer parties, and it's one my mum would always cook when the sun came out and the smoky coals of the barbecue were calling. It's one of her favorite sunshine dishes, and it's also a great vegan option. Mum used to cook this straight on the barbecue, but it works just as well in the oven. I was a little worried about the transition to the slow cooker—surprisingly, it works really well. All I can say is that they are very filling, so go easy!

4 medium Yukon Gold potatoes

2 red bell peppers

2 green bell peppers

1 teaspoon rapeseed oil

1 teaspoon cumin seeds

1 cup frozen peas

1 teaspoon salt

1 fresh green chile, finely chopped

1 teaspoon Garam Masala (page 23)

1 tablespoon fenugreek leaves

1-inch (3-cm) piece fresh ginger, grated

1 tablespoon fresh coriander leaves, finely chopped

1. Boil the potatoes with the skin on until they're soft (about 15 minutes), then leave to cool. (I always boil potatoes with the skin on, as it stops them taking on too much water and becoming mushy.) Peel off their skins and dice the potatoes.

2. Preheat the slow cooker on high and make sure the 4 peppers will fit into the cooker side by side.

3. Heat the oil in a small frying pan, and then toast the cumin seeds until fragrant, about 1 minute. Add the peas to soften.

4. Put the toasted cumin and peas in a large bowl. Then add the cooked potatoes with the salt, chile, garam masala, fenugreek leaves, ginger, and fresh coriander leaves, and mix together. Taste the filling and adjust the seasoning.

5. Slice the tops off the peppers, keeping the stalks intact. Remove the seeds and discard. Divide the potato mixture into 4 portions and stuff each of the peppers.

6. If you have a tray for the inside of your slow cooker, place this inside. If not, crumple up some foil to make a little tray for the peppers to sit on.

7. Place the stuffed peppers on the tray inside the cooker. Replace the top of each of the peppers. Pour about ¼ to ⅓ cup (50 to 100 mL) of water into the cooker outside of the tray (so the peppers are not sitting in the water).

8. Cook on low for 4 hours, or for 2 hours on high.

SIMPLE SUBSTITUTION: If you want a bit of meat in this dish, replace the potatoes with minced lamb. Brown and drain the meat before adding it to the stuffing mixture.

Coconut Quinoa Curry

Kosambari Masala

⚙ QUICK PREP ⓥ VEGAN | SERVES 6
PREP TIME: 5 MINUTES | COOK TIME: 6 HOURS ON LOW OR 3 TO 4 HOURS ON HIGH

Kosambar is a South Indian salad made with moong dhal. For this recipe I have substituted quinoa and added chickpeas to make a heartier dish high in nutritional value. It's a fabulous choice for the slow cooker. Quinoa is a super grain that cooks beautifully with this method, and it's an excellent protein source that contains essential amino acids and is high in magnesium, iron, and fiber. Make sure to take leftovers to work for lunch. Don't be discouraged if your cooker looks half empty when you turn it on. Quinoa quadruples in size when cooked.

2 cups coconut milk

1 cup uncooked quinoa

⅓ cup (100 mL) hot water

1 (14-ounce/400-g) can chickpeas, drained and rinsed

1 tablespoon tomato purée

1 tablespoon freshly grated ginger

1 teaspoon turmeric

1 teaspoon chili powder

1 teaspoon sea salt

2 garlic cloves, minced

1 sweet potato, peeled and chopped

1 large broccoli crown, cut into florets

1 tomato, diced

1 fresh green chile, chopped

½ white onion, finely diced (about 1 cup)

Shredded fresh coconut, for garnish

Handful fresh coriander leaves, chopped

1. Wash the quinoa in a few changes of water to rid it of its external coating, which can be bitter.

2. Add all ingredients except the shredded coconut and the coriander leaves to the slow cooker, and stir until everything is mixed.

3. Cover and cook on high for 3 to 4 hours, or for 6 hours on low, until the sweet potato is cooked through. Stir halfway through cooking, if you can.

4. Top with coconut shreds and coriander leaves, and serve hot.

SIMPLE SUBSTITUTION: You can use peeled butternut squash, or any hard winter squash, instead of sweet potato.

South Indian Cabbage Fry
Cabbage Thoran

⚙ QUICK PREP Ⓥ VEGAN | SERVES 6

PREP TIME: 10 MINUTES | COOK TIME: 3 HOURS ON LOW OR 1 HOUR ON HIGH

In Kerala, *thoran* is a generic term used for a dry vegetable curry that can literally be made with any of the local, seasonal vegetables. Keralan cuisine uses a lot of green vegetables, such as snake beans, tindori, and ivy berries. Unripe jackfruit is also common, along with leafy greens. I have used cabbage here because I love it and think that spicing up simple green vegetables is a quick, healthy, and delicious way to use them. Plus, it works well in the slow cooker.

3 tablespoons coconut oil

2 teaspoons black mustard seeds

2 tablespoons chopped fresh curry leaves

1 teaspoon cumin seeds

2 dried Kashmiri chiles, broken into small pieces

2-inch (5-cm) piece fresh ginger, finely grated

½ teaspoon turmeric

1 teaspoon salt

½ teaspoon freshly ground black pepper

4 cups shredded savoy cabbage

2 fresh green chiles, sliced

½ cup freshly grated coconut

¼ cup (50 mL) water

Juice of 1 lemon

1. Heat the oil in a frying pan (or in the slow cooker if you have a sear setting). Add the mustard seeds, followed by the curry leaves, cumin seeds, and dried chiles. Sauté until the spices sizzle and become aromatic, about 30 seconds.

2. Pour into the slow cooker. Add the ginger, turmeric, salt, and black pepper. Stir in the cabbage, green chiles, fresh coconut, and water.

3. Cover and cook on low for 3 hours, or on high for 1 hour.

4. When the dish is cooked, squeeze in the lemon juice. Mix and serve with fresh boiled rice.

Vegetable Vindaloo

Tarkari Vindahlo

Ⓥ VEGAN | SERVES 6

PREP TIME: 15 MINUTES | COOK TIME: 3 TO 4 HOURS ON LOW OR 2 HOURS ON HIGH

This is my vegan version of the classic Goan vindaloo, which is usually cooked with pork. The spice paste is robust and the flavors work well with these vegetables, but you can use other vegetables if you prefer. I have included kidney beans to give the dish some substance. The classic vindaloo is famous for being the hottest dish on most restaurant menus, but you can tweak the chile types and amounts to suit your taste. Most important for achieving a fantastic flavor is balancing the vinegar, chile, and sweetness.

FOR THE SPICE PASTE

1 teaspoon mustard seeds

1 teaspoon cumin seeds

2 teaspoons coriander seeds

4 cloves

4 dried Kashmiri chiles

1 teaspoon black peppercorns

2 onions, roughly chopped

6 garlic cloves

1-inch (3-cm) piece fresh ginger

4 tablespoons malt vinegar

FOR THE VINDALOO

1 tablespoon vegetable oil

1 teaspoon mustard seeds

4 medium potatoes, peeled and cut into 1-inch (3-cm) cubes

4 ounces (100 g) cauliflower florets

1 zucchini, diced

4 ounces (100 g) mushrooms, sliced

1 carrot, peeled and sliced

1 (14-ounce/400-g) can kidney beans, drained and rinsed

1 teaspoon salt

1 teaspoon turmeric

½ teaspoon sugar

TO MAKE THE SPICE PASTE

1. Preheat the slow cooker on high for 15 minutes.

2. In a blender, make the spice paste by grinding the mustard seeds, cumin seeds, coriander seeds, cloves, chiles, and peppercorns to a fine powder.

3. Then add the onions, garlic, ginger, vinegar, and a splash of water to the powder. Blend to make a paste.

TO MAKE THE VINDALOO

1. Heat the oil in a frying pan (or in the slow cooker if you have a sear setting). Add the mustard seeds and cook until they pop. Add all of the spice paste and cook until the paste is fragrant.

2. Put everything in the slow cooker. Add the potatoes, cauliflower florets, zucchini, mushrooms, carrot, and beans. Then stir in the salt, turmeric, and sugar, plus a splash of water if needed.

3. Cover and cook on low for 3 to 4 hours, or on high for 2 hours.

4. Check the seasoning and adjust if required. Serve hot.

Old Delhi Butter Chicken *page 110*

Chicken

Chapter Seven

Quick-Fried Spicy Chicken
Murgh Jalfrezi

SERVES 6

PREP TIME: 15 MINUTES | COOK TIME: 6 HOURS ON LOW OR 4 HOURS ON HIGH

Jal means "quick" and frezi is "fry" or "spice." This is a spicy quick-fry, even when cooked in the slow cooker. You leave the chicken to slow cook until it soaks up the spices, and then, just before serving the dish, do a 2-minute quick-fry of the bell peppers. It's healthier than fried chicken, but just as savory, and the peppers provide an irresistible crunch.

FOR THE CHICKEN

2 tablespoons rapeseed oil

4 fresh green chiles, chopped

4 garlic cloves, sliced

4 tomatoes, chopped

1 teaspoon salt

½ teaspoon turmeric

8 boneless chicken thighs, skinned, trimmed, and cut into chunks

¼ cup water

FOR THE QUICK-FRY

1 tablespoon rapeseed oil

1 teaspoon cumin seeds

1 red onion, sliced

1 red bell pepper, seeded and cut into chunks

1 green bell pepper, seeded and cut into chunks

2 fresh green chiles, sliced lengthwise

1 tomato, chopped

½ teaspoon salt

1 teaspoon Garam Masala (page 23)

TO MAKE THE CHICKEN

1. Heat the slow cooker to high and add the oil.

2. Add the chiles, garlic, chopped tomatoes, salt, and turmeric, and cook for a few minutes. Add the chicken pieces and the water. Then stir to coat the chicken.

3. Cover and cook on high for 4 hours, or on low for 6 hours.

TO MAKE THE QUICK-FRY

1. When you are ready to eat, heat the oil in a sauté pan and add the cumin seeds. Cook until fragrant, about 1 minute.

2. Add the onion, red and green pepper chunks, chiles, tomato, salt, and garam masala, and sauté for 5 minutes.

3. Add this pepper mixture to the chicken in the slow cooker, cover, and cook on high for another 15 minutes with the cover off, until the peppers are cooked to your taste and the sauce has reduced and thickened.

EASY ADJUSTMENT: You can cook the peppers as much or as little as you like. I prefer mine with a bit of a crunch, and that's what this recipe will give you. If you prefer your peppers soft, you can cook everything in the slow cooker with the chicken. And if you want them barely cooked, just stir the peppers into the chicken after the quick-fry, and serve the dish.

Spicy Pulled Chicken
Chaat Murgh

 QUICK PREP | SERVES 4

PREP TIME: 5 MINUTES | COOK TIME: 6 HOURS ON LOW OR 4 HOURS ON HIGH

Chaat means "lick," and it refers to dishes that have a lip-smacking delicious-ness. This dish is all about that wonderful Moorish, piquant flavor that is achieved by the unique balance of sweet, spicy, hot, and sour flavors. In the slow cooker, this makes an amazing pulled-chicken dish that you just have to try. Serve with some yogurt all wrapped up in a Whole-Wheat Flatbread (page 181).

8 chicken thighs, skinned and trimmed

4 garlic cloves

1 teaspoon salt

1 onion, finely sliced

2 fresh green chiles, finely chopped

2 to 4 tablespoons tamarind paste

1 teaspoon chili powder

1 teaspoon mango powder (amchoor)

1 tablespoon jaggery (or dark-brown sugar)

1 cup (250 mL) water

1 teaspoon Garam Masala (page 23)

Handful fresh coriander leaves, chopped

1 teaspoon Chaat Masala (page 23, optional)

1. Preheat the slow cooker on high.

2. Place the chicken, garlic, salt, onion, chiles, tamarind, chili powder, mango powder, jaggery, and water in the cooker. Cover and cook for 4 hours on high, or for 6 to 8 hours on low.

3. Remove the chicken. Using two forks, shred the chicken.

4. The sauce should be nice and thick. If you want to reduce it a bit more, turn the cooker to high and cook with the lid off for 15 or 20 minutes longer, until you are happy with the consis-tency. Pour the sauce from the cooker onto the meat.

5. Sprinkle with some garam masala, fresh coriander leaves, and chaat masala (if using), and serve.

- -

PORTION TIP: This recipe can easily be doubled, so make extra for leftovers. Use what's left for a delicious sandwich filling, or stir it into couscous for a quick-and-easy lunch. I would not double the amount of tamarind paste during cooking, to make sure it doesn't become too piquant. You can always add more after it's cooked.

Cumin-Spiced Chicken Wings

Jeera Wings

QUICK PREP | SERVES 6

PREP TIME: 5 MINUTES | COOK TIME: 6 HOURS ON LOW OR 4 HOURS ON HIGH

What do Buffalo wings and Indian food have in common? They're typically eaten at restaurants and as takeout. Most people love Buffalo wings, but you may have been avoiding them because they're deep fried. These great cumin-flavored Buffalo chicken wings start off in the slow cooker—making them healthier—and for ultimate crispiness, can be finished off in the oven.

3 tablespoons rapeseed oil

2 teaspoons ground cumin seeds, ground

2 teaspoons crushed garlic

2 teaspoons freshly grated ginger

1 teaspoon cumin seeds

1 teaspoon salt

1 teaspoon coriander seeds, ground

1 teaspoon chili powder

2 fresh green chiles, finely sliced

24 chicken wings

Handful fresh coriander leaves, chopped

Juice of 1 lemon

1 teaspoon red chili flakes (optional)

1. Preheat the slow cooker on high.

2. Mix all of the ingredients except for the coriander leaves, lemon juice, and chili flakes in a bowl, and add the wings. Toss well to coat them.

3. Place the wings in the slow cooker. Cover and cook them on low for 6 hours, or on high for 4 hours.

4. To serve, garnish with fresh coriander leaves, a squeeze of lemon, and some chili flakes (if using).

EASY ADJUSTMENT: If you want to crisp up the wings, place them on a flat, lightly oiled baking sheet in a hot oven (400°F, or 200°C) for 10 to 20 minutes, just before serving.

Old Delhi Butter Chicken

Murgh Makhani

SERVES 6

PREP TIME: 15 MINUTES | **COOK TIME: 7 HOURS ON LOW OR 3 TO 4 HOURS ON HIGH**

Murgh makhani is a classic restaurant dish that is silky, smooth, and beautifully luxurious. The complex flavors include the natural sweetness of honey, the earthy bitter undertones of fenugreek leaves, the creaminess of makhan (butter), and the tang of fresh tomatoes. All combine to produce a thick, rich sauce that's North Indian through and through. Many restaurants have the luxury of marinating the chicken pieces and cooking them in the tandoor before adding them to the decadent sauce—not always possible at home. This is my interpretation of how you can make this classic in a slow cooker. Yes, it's a two-stage process, but the result is fantastic!

FOR THE TOMATO SAUCE

3 medium red onions, roughly chopped

2 to 3 fresh green chiles

1 tablespoon freshly grated ginger

6 garlic cloves, roughly chopped

2¾-inch (7-cm) piece cassia bark

5 green cardamom pods

4 cloves

10 black peppercorns

1 teaspoon salt

10 ripe red tomatoes, roughly chopped, or 1 (14-ounce/400-g) can plum tomatoes

1 tablespoon tomato paste

½ teaspoon turmeric

1 tablespoon Kashmiri chili powder

2 teaspoons coriander seeds, ground

2 cups hot water

FOR THE CHICKEN

2 tablespoons ghee or butter

1 tablespoon cumin seeds

12 chicken thighs, skinned, trimmed, and cut into cubes

1 to 2 tablespoons honey

1 tablespoon dried fenugreek leaves

⅓ cup (100 mL) heavy cream (optional)

1 tablespoon butter (optional)

Coriander leaves to garnish (optional)

TO MAKE THE TOMATO SAUCE

1. Heat the slow cooker to high and add the onion, chiles, ginger, garlic, cassia bark, green cardamom pods, cloves, black peppercorns, salt, tomatoes, tomato paste, turmeric, chili powder, ground coriander seeds, and water.

2. Cover and cook on high for 1 to 2 hours, or on low for 3 hours. By the end, the tomatoes should have broken down.

3. Remove the cassia bark (this is important, because if you grind the cassia in the sauce it will turn out much darker) and blend the sauce with an immersion or regular blender until it's smooth. You can strain this to get a fine, glossy sauce, if you'd like, or leave it as it is. Return the sauce to the slow cooker.

TO MAKE THE CHICKEN

1. In a frying pan, heat the ghee. Add cumin seeds and cook until fragrant, about 1 minute. Pour into the sauce in the slow cooker.

2. Add the diced chicken, cover the slow cooker, and cook on high for 2 hours, or on low for 4 hours.

3. When the chicken is cooked, stir in the honey, dried fenugreek leaves, and cream (if using). If you want to thicken the sauce you can turn the cooker to high and reduce for a while with the cover off. Add some butter, a little extra drizzle of cream, and garnish with coriander leaves (if using) just before serving.

EASY ADJUSTMENT: You can also marinate the chicken in a tandoori-style marinade (as on page 112) and cook it in the oven, and then add it to the tomato sauce in this recipe. It's also the perfect sauce to have with paneer. Once the paneer is added (step 2 in the section "To make the chicken"), it will only need about 15 minutes of cooking on high, just to heat through.

Whole Tandoori-Style Braised Chicken
Tandoori Masala Murgh

 QUICK PREP | **SERVES 6**

PREP TIME: 10 MINUTES, PLUS TIME TO MARINATE | **COOK TIME: 6 TO 8 HOURS ON LOW OR 4 HOURS ON HIGH**

I love tandoori chicken, which is usually cooked in a tandoor oven, making the meat succulent, tender, and smoky. This is an adaptation of that tandoori style using a similar marinade but a very different cooking method. The Kashmiri chili powder is essential, giving that lovely orange-red color this dish is well known for. For a less-heated alternative, replace half of the chili powder with paprika. Make sure the chicken fits whole in your slow cooker—if not, cut it into quarters. Serve this dish with a sliced red-onion salad and some Mint Chutney (page 170).

1 tablespoon freshly grated ginger

5 garlic cloves, minced

2 fresh green chiles, finely chopped

⅔ cup (150 mL) Greek yogurt

2 tablespoons mustard oil

1 tablespoon Kashmiri chili powder

1 tablespoon dried fenugreek leaves

1 tablespoon gram flour

2 teaspoons Garam Masala (page 23)

1 teaspoon sea salt

1 teaspoon ground cumin

Juice of 1 large lemon

1 whole chicken, about 3⅓ pounds (1½ kg)

Handful fresh coriander leaves, chopped

1. Put the ginger, garlic, and green chiles in a spice grinder and grind to a paste. Empty into a large bowl and stir in all the other ingredients, except for the chicken and the coriander leaves.

2. Skin the chicken. Then, using a sharp knife, slash the chicken breasts and legs to allow the marinade to penetrate.

3. Marinate in the refrigerator for as long as you can leave it. (Overnight is fine.)

4. Preheat the slow cooker on high. My cooker has a stand I can sit meat on, but if you don't have one, scrunch up some foil and put it in the bottom of the cooker. Pour a few tablespoons of water in the bottom of the cooker and place the chicken on the foil.

5. Cook on high for 4 hours, or on low for 6 to 8 hours.

6. Remove the chicken from the cooker and cut it into pieces. Sprinkle the chopped coriander leaves over the chicken and serve.

EASY ADJUSTMENT: Once the chicken is cooked, if you want to mimic the tandoor flavor, you can finish the meat off in a hot oven. Place the chicken on a baking sheet and cook at 400°F (200°C) for 10 to 20 minutes, just to char it.

Fenugreek Chicken
Methi Murgh

 QUICK PREP | SERVES 6

PREP TIME: 10 MINUTES | **COOK TIME: 6 HOURS ON LOW OR 4 HOURS ON HIGH, PLUS ½ HOUR ON HIGH**

Methi is fenugreek, an herb similar to clover. It's native to the Mediterranean, Southern Europe, and Western Asia. The leaves have a subtle bitterness, although the seeds are slightly sweet. This dish has an amazing flavor that will leave you wanting to soak up the sauce with lots of Whole-Wheat Flatbread (page 181). To make the most of this dish, brown the onions first (you can even do so the night before)—I urge you!

1 tablespoon vegetable oil

2 teaspoons cumin seeds

2 onions, finely diced

2 tablespoons freshly grated ginger

3 garlic cloves, finely chopped

1 teaspoon turmeric

2 tomatoes, puréed

1 teaspoon chili powder

1 teaspoon coriander seeds, ground

1 teaspoon salt

1 or 2 fresh green chiles, chopped

8 boneless chicken thighs, skinned, trimmed, and cut into chunks

2 bunches fresh fenugreek leaves, washed and finely chopped (or 3 tablespoons dried fenugreek leaves)

2 tablespoons yogurt

2 teaspoons Garam Masala (page 23)

1. Heat the oil in a frying pan (or in the slow cooker if you have a sear setting). Add the cumin seeds. Once fragrant, add the onions and cook until they begin to brown, about 10 minutes. Add the ginger, garlic, and turmeric, and cook for a few minutes.

2. Stir in the puréed tomatoes, chili powder, ground coriander seeds, salt, and green chiles. Put everything in the slow cooker and set the cooker to high.

3. Stir in the chicken pieces. Cover and cook on high for 4 hours, or on low for 6 hours.

4. Add the fenugreek leaves and stir into the sauce. Leave the cover off and cook for another half hour on high. This will also reduce the sauce and thicken it slightly.

5. Turn the cooker to low and stir in the yogurt, 1 tablespoon at a time, until it's fully incorporated into the sauce.

6. Turn off the heat, stir in the garam masala, and serve.

EASY ADJUSTMENT: For a thicker sauce, switch the slow cooker to the sear mode when the cooking is done, and continue to cook, stirring, until the sauce becomes thick and clings to the meat. This can also be done in a separate pan on the stove.

Chettinad Chicken

SERVES 6

PREP TIME: 15 MINUTES | COOK TIME: 6 HOURS ON LOW OR 4 HOURS ON HIGH

This chicken curry dish from Tamil Nadu in South India has a very complex layering of flavors. Toasting the spices with the coconut produces a delicious, aromatic masala with an aniseed scent from the fennel seeds. Think it might be too fiery? Just reduce the number of dried red chiles. If white poppy seeds are hard to find then black can be used.

1 tablespoon white poppy seeds

1 teaspoon coriander seeds

2 teaspoons cumin seeds

1 teaspoon fennel seeds

4 to 5 dried red chiles

2-inch (5-cm) piece cinnamon stick

6 green cardamom pods

4 cloves

1½ cups grated coconut

4 garlic cloves

1 tablespoon freshly grated ginger

2 tablespoons coconut oil

20 curry leaves

3 onions, finely sliced

2 star anise

4 tomatoes

1 teaspoon turmeric

Sea salt

1 teaspoon chili powder

12 chicken thighs on the bone, skinned and trimmed

Juice of 2 or 3 limes

Handful fresh coriander leaves, chopped

1. In a frying pan, toast the poppy seeds, coriander seeds, cumin seeds, fennel seeds, dried red chiles, cinnamon, green cardamom pods, and cloves until fragrant, about 1 minute. Remove from the pan and set aside to cool. Once cooled, grind to a fine powder in a spice grinder.

2. In the same pan, toast the grated coconut for 3 to 4 minutes until it just starts to turn golden. Remove from the pan and spread on a plate to cool. Once cooled, grind and mix with the ground spices.

3. Crush the garlic and ginger in a mortar and pestle and set aside.

4. Either heat the slow cooker to sauté or use a pan on the stove. Heat the coconut oil and add the curry leaves, when they stop spluttering, add the sliced onions and fry them until they are light brown. Stir in the crushed garlic and ginger, and stir for a minute or two.

5. Add to the slow cooker along with the ground spices and anise. Chop and add the tomatoes, the turmeric, and the salt, and stir in the chili powder.

6. Place the chicken pieces in the cooker, cover and cook on low for 6 hours, or on high for 4 hours, until tender and cooked through.

7. Check the seasoning and adjust if needed, squeeze in the lime juice, and serve topped with fresh coriander leaves.

TECHNIQUE TIP: It's important to remove the spices and coconut from the hot pan right away, or they will continue to cook and could burn. Spread them on a plate to cool before grinding.

Punjabi Chicken Curry
Thari Wala

SERVES 6

PREP TIME: 20 MINUTES | COOK TIME: 6 HOURS ON LOW OR 4 HOURS ON HIGH

This was the first chicken curry dish I ever cooked, and today it's a family favorite. Thari wala translates to "chicken in a sauce." It's usually cooked with the meat on the bone, which results in a delicious, rich gravy—and mopping it up with Whole-Wheat Flatbread (page 181) or Naan (page 184) is pure pleasure. I can remember that it was my dad's job to skin and chop the chicken while my mum focused on making the thick, robust masala base. It may seem like a basic dish with simple ingredients, but it is packed full of flavor. It's my classic chicken curry dish, and thankfully, it's superb made in the slow cooker!

2 tablespoons vegetable oil

3 onions, finely diced

6 garlic cloves, finely chopped

1 heaped tablespoon freshly grated ginger

1 (14-ounce/400-g) can plum tomatoes

1 teaspoon salt

1 teaspoon turmeric

1 teaspoon chili powder

Handful coriander stems, finely chopped

3 fresh green chiles, finely chopped

12 pieces chicken, mixed thighs and drumsticks, or a whole chicken, skinned, trimmed, and chopped

2 teaspoons Garam Masala (page 23)

Handful fresh coriander leaves, chopped

1. Heat the oil in a frying pan (or in the slow cooker if you have a sear setting). Add the diced onions and cook for 5 minutes. Add the garlic and continue to cook for 10 minutes until the onions are brown.

2. Heat the slow cooker to high and add the onion-and-garlic mixture. Stir in the ginger, tomatoes, salt, turmeric, chili powder, coriander stems, and chiles.

3. Add the chicken pieces. Cover and cook on low for 6 hours, or on high for 4 hours.

4. Once cooked, check the seasoning, and then stir in the garam masala and coriander leaves.

- -

EASY ADJUSTMENT: If you prefer more sauce, you can add some boiling water to the gravy after it's cooked. Add just a little at a time and stir well to loosen the gravy. This recipe also works well with trimmed lamb loin chops or bone-in shoulder chops (cut into bite-size pieces, but use the bone as well)—only increase the cooking time to 6 hours on low.

Coconut Curry Chicken

Nariyal Murgh

SERVES 6

PREP TIME: 15 MINUTES | COOK TIME: 4 HOURS ON LOW OR 3 HOURS ON HIGH

Nariyal is the Hindi word for "coconut." This is a bit of a hybrid dish, with a base sauce from the North but coconut flavor from the South. It's a creamy chicken dish that doesn't need any ginger or garlic, and it's packed full of flavor despite not having many ingredients. A perfect midweek curry—serve simply with Plain Basmati Rice (page 180).

1 tablespoon coconut oil

1 teaspoon cumin seeds

2 medium onions, grated

7 to 8 ounces (200 g) canned plum tomatoes

1 teaspoon salt

1 teaspoon turmeric

½ to 1 teaspoon Kashmiri chili powder (optional)

2 to 3 fresh green chiles, chopped

1 cup (250 mL) coconut cream

12 chicken thighs, skinned, trimmed, and cut into bite-size chunks

1 teaspoon Garam Masala (page 23)

Handful fresh coriander leaves, chopped

1. Heat the oil in a frying pan (or in the slow cooker if you have a sear setting). Add the cumin seeds. When sizzling and aromatic, add the onions and cook until they are browning, about 5 to 7 minutes.

2. In a blender, purée the tomatoes and add them to the pan with the salt, turmeric, chili powder (if using), and fresh green chiles.

3. Stir together and put everything in the slow cooker. Pour in the coconut cream. Add the meat and stir to coat with the sauce.

4. Cover and cook on low for 4 hours, or on high for 3 hours.

5. Taste the sauce and adjust the seasoning. If the sauce is very liquidy, turn the cooker to high and cook for 30 minutes more with the lid off.

6. Add the garam masala and throw in the fresh coriander leaves to serve.

TECHNIQUE TIP: If grating onions makes you cry, use a food processor or even a blender. Pulse lightly so they don't get too mushy.

Hot Goan-Style Coconut Chicken
Xacuti Murgh

SERVES 6

PREP TIME: 20 MINUTES | COOK TIME: 6 HOURS ON LOW OR 4 HOURS ON HIGH

Chicken xacuti or shakuti is a unique South Indian dish, from the state of Goa, that is made with poppy seeds and Kashmiri chiles. It's thought that the word comes from the Portuguese *chacuti*, which indeed is a bit similar to this. The chicken is marinated in a fragrant paste created from roasted and ground spices. The beautiful bright-red color comes from the lovely Kashmiri chiles, a key ingredient of this dish. If you're looking to stimulate your taste buds, this meal is for you—hot, fiery, and delicious.

FOR THE SPICE PASTE

8 dried Kashmiri chiles, broken into pieces

2 tablespoons coriander seeds

2-inch (5-cm) piece cassia bark, broken into pieces

1 teaspoon black peppercorns

1 teaspoon cumin seeds

1 teaspoon fennel seeds

4 cloves

2 star anise

1 tablespoon poppy seeds

1 cup freshly grated coconut, or desiccated coconut shreds

6 garlic cloves

⅓ cup (100 mL) water

FOR THE CHICKEN

12 chicken thigh and drumstick pieces, on the bone, skinless

1 teaspoon salt (or to taste)

1 teaspoon turmeric

2 tablespoons coconut oil

2 medium onions, finely sliced

⅓ cup (100 mL) water

½ teaspoon ground nutmeg

2 teaspoons tamarind paste

Handful fresh coriander leaves, chopped for garnish

1 or 2 fresh red chiles, for garnish

TO MAKE THE SPICE PASTE

1. In a dry frying pan, roast the Kashmiri chiles, coriander seeds, cassia bark, peppercorns, cumin seeds, fennel seeds, cloves, and star anise until fragrant, about 1 minute. Add the poppy seeds and continue roasting for a few minutes. Then remove from the heat and leave to cool.

2. Once cooled, grind the toasted spices in your spice grinder and set aside.

3. In the same pan, add the dried coconut and toast it for 5 to 7 minutes, until it just starts to turn golden.

4. Transfer to a blender with the garlic, and add the water. Blend to make a thick, wet paste.

5. Add the ground spices and blend again to mix together.

TO MAKE THE CHICKEN

1. In a large bowl, toss the chicken with the salt and turmeric. Marinate for 15 to 20 minutes. In the meantime, heat the slow cooker to high.

2. Heat the oil in a frying pan (or in the slow cooker if you have a sear setting). Cook the sliced onions for 10 minutes, and then add the spice and coconut paste. Cook until it becomes fragrant.

3. Transfer everything to the slow cooker. Add the chicken, then the water. Cover and cook on low for 6 hours, or on high for 4 hours.

4. Sprinkle in the nutmeg and stir in the tamarind paste. Cover and cook for another 5 minutes.

5. Garnish with fresh coriander leaves and whole red chiles to serve.

INGREDIENT TIP: Kashmiri chiles are my chiles and chili powder of choice. They grow in the Kashmir region and are big and wrinkly when dried. They have a musky, smoky aroma and a mildish heat, resulting in a wonderful flavor. What I love about them the most is the color they impart—a beautiful, vibrant red—which is perfect for dishes like this one, for tandoori, and for rogan josh. They're available online and at most Indian grocery stores. If you're unable to purchase any, a great substitution for Kashmiri chili powder is using a blend of equal parts smoked paprika and chili powder.

Chicken Korma

 CONTAINS NUTS | SERVES 6

PREP TIME: 20 MINUTES, PLUS TIME TO MARINATE | COOK TIME: 4 HOURS ON LOW
OR 3 HOURS ON HIGH

A classic korma is a regal dish where the meat or vegetables are braised with
yogurt or cream and combined with spices, producing a thick sauce. A decadent restaurant-classic favorite, the creamy coconut and almonds give this
korma a delicious fragrance and natural sweetness. Rather than being heavy
and sweet like a restaurant korma, this dish is fresh and uplifting. I love the
creamy coconut, but I prefer my korma with a chile kick, so I added some dried
chile to the ingredients. If you don't have saffron on hand, it's okay to just
leave it out.

FOR THE MARINADE

1 tablespoon coriander
seeds, ground

1 teaspoon salt

6 whole black
peppercorns

1-inch (3-cm) piece fresh
ginger, roughly chopped

3 garlic cloves,
roughly chopped

12 boneless chicken
thighs, skinned and
chopped into chunks

1 cup Greek yogurt

1 heaped teaspoon
gram flour

1 teaspoon turmeric

FOR THE KORMA

1 tablespoon ghee or
vegetable oil

3 cloves

3 green cardamom pods

1-inch (3-cm) piece
cassia bark

1 to 3 dried red chiles

2 onions, minced

⅓ cup creamed coconut

2 heaped tablespoons
ground almonds

1 teaspoon ground white
poppy seeds

Pinch of saffron

2 tablespoons milk

1 teaspoon Garam Masala
(page 23)

Handful fresh coriander
leaves, finely chopped

1 tablespoon chopped
toasted almonds

Squeeze of lemon juice

TO MAKE THE MARINADE

1. Place the coriander seeds, salt, and peppercorns into a mortar and pestle and crush, or grind them in a spice grinder. Then add the roughly chopped ginger and garlic, and pound (or grind) to create an aromatic paste.

2. Place the chicken in a large bowl and add the yogurt, gram flour, turmeric, and spice paste. Stir thoroughly, cover, and leave to marinate for an hour, or longer if possible, in the refrigerator.

TO MAKE THE KORMA

1. Heat the slow cooker to high and add the oil. Add the cloves, cardamom pods, cassia bark, and the dried red chiles, and toast until fragrant, about 1 minute.

2. Add the minced onions, and then add the marinated chicken. Cover and cook for 2 hours on low, or for 1 hour on high.

3. Pour in the creamed coconut, ground almonds, and poppy seeds, then stir. Cover and cook on low for 2 more hours.

4. Crumble the saffron into a small bowl, add the milk, and leave to steep for 20 minutes.

5. Once cooked through and the sauce has thickened, pour in the saffron milk for added decadence, if using. Then add the garam masala. Garnish with the fresh coriander leaves and chopped almonds. You can also add a squeeze of lemon juice for added freshness, then serve.

SUBSTITUTION TIP: You can use 1¾ cups (400 mL) of coconut milk instead of the coconut cream. But coconut cream will give you a fuller, richer flavor.

Chicken Tikka Masala

CONTAINS NUTS | SERVES 6

PREP TIME: 20 MINUTES, PLUS TIME TO MARINATE | COOK TIME: 4 HOURS ON LOW OR 3 HOURS ON HIGH

This is a favorite worldwide. It's traditionally made with marinated chicken cooked in a tandoor oven, then soaked in a delicious tomato sauce. I've simplified the preparation process a bit for the slow cooker, but you can still make an amazing masala and either precook the chicken before adding it to the sauce, or do the whole thing in the slow cooker—it will be delicious either way.

FOR THE MARINADE

3 tablespoons Greek yogurt

1 heaped teaspoon fenugreek seeds

1 teaspoon chili powder

1 teaspoon coriander seeds, ground

1 teaspoon gram flour

½ teaspoon salt

1-inch (3-cm) piece fresh ginger

3 garlic cloves

Juice of 1 lime

FOR THE MASALA

2-inch (5-cm) piece cassia bark

3 green cardamom pods

2 bay leaves

3 cloves

1 teaspoon cumin seeds

1 tablespoon rapeseed oil

1 large onion, minced or very finely diced

1 tablespoon minced ginger

3 garlic cloves, minced

2 teaspoons cumin seeds

2 teaspoons coriander seeds

1 teaspoon chili powder

1 teaspoon salt

½ teaspoon turmeric

1 to 2 tablespoons raw, unsalted cashews

3 fresh tomatoes

FOR THE CHICKEN

8 boneless chicken thighs, skinned and cut into large chunks

1 red bell pepper, cut into large chunks

1 red onion, cut into large chunks

2 tablespoons mustard oil

1 teaspoon dried fenugreek leaves

⅓ cup (100 mL) heavy cream

Handful fresh coriander leaves, chopped

TO MAKE THE MARINADE

1. In a large bowl, mix together all of the ingredients until well blended.

2. Add the chicken, bell pepper, and red onion, and toss to coat.

3. Cover and set aside for half an hour to marinate.

TO MAKE THE MASALA

1. Heat the slow cooker to high and add the cassia bark, cardamom pods, bay leaves, cloves, and cumin seeds. Toast lightly until fragrant, about 1 minute.

2. In a frying pan, heat the oil, and then add the onions and cook gently for 10 minutes, until golden. Stir in the ginger and garlic for a minute, and then transfer to the slow cooker.

3. Crush the cumin and coriander seeds (or grind in your spice grinder) and stir them into the pan with the chili powder, salt, and turmeric.

4. Grind the cashew nuts to a powder in your spice grinder. Transfer the powder to a blender or food processor, add the tomatoes, and purée. Add this to the slow cooker.

5. Cover and cook on low for 4 hours, or on high for 3 hours.

TO MAKE THE CHICKEN

1. An hour before the masala is finished, place the marinated chicken, red bell pepper, and onion in a large, flat baking dish and pour the mustard oil over everything. Roast for 30 minutes at 350ºF (180ºC), until the chicken pieces are a little charred around the edges.

2. Transfer the chicken, vegetables, and any pan juices into the slow cooker for the final 30 minutes.

3. Add the dried fenugreek leaves, pour in a little cream, and stir in the coriander leaves to serve.

TECHNIQUE TIP: If you don't want to cook the chicken in the oven first, you can marinate it and then add it straight into the slow cooker for the full cooking time.

Slow-Cooked Lamb Shanks *page 136*

Lamb, Pork, and Beef

Minted Indian Meatballs

Kofta Curry

SERVES 6 TO 8

PREP TIME: 20 MINUTES | COOK TIME: 4 HOURS ON LOW OR 2 TO 3 HOURS ON HIGH

This is a big family favorite in my home, and it's the first dish my daughter ever cooked on her own. The kofta are little spice bombs packed with flavor all nestled in a light, delicious gravy. If you prefer a thicker sauce, reduce the amount of water by half.

1¾ pounds (800 g) lean ground lamb

2 teaspoons ground cumin

2 teaspoons chili powder, divided

3 teaspoons Garam Masala (page 23)

Handful fresh mint, chopped

½ teaspoon ground cinnamon

2 teaspoons salt, divided

2 large onions

6 garlic cloves

2-inch (5-cm) piece fresh ginger

2 to 3 fresh green chiles

1 (14-ounce/400-g) can plum tomatoes

1 tablespoon rapeseed oil

1 teaspoon turmeric

1 teaspoon dried fenugreek leaves

1 to 1¼ cups (250 to 300 mL) hot water

Handful fresh coriander leaves, finely chopped

1. In a large mixing bowl, add the lamb, cumin, 1 teaspoon chili powder, garam masala, mint, cinnamon, and 1 teaspoon of salt. Mix well using your hands to ensure the spices are evenly distributed.

2. Rub a little oil on your hands to prevent the meat from sticking to them. Then take a small amount of the meat and roll it in your palms to make a meatball. Make sure it is smooth all over. Set aside and repeat with the remaining mixture. You should get about 24 kofta.

3. In a blender, mince the onions, garlic, ginger, and chiles—not to a purée, just so everything is chopped—and set aside. Blend the tomatoes to a purée.

4. Heat the slow cooker to high and add the oil. Carefully fry the kofta in batches so they brown all over. Remove the kofta and set them on some paper towels to drain.

5. Add the onion mixture to the cooker and cook for 5 to 6 minutes in the remaining oil. Add the tomatoes, turmeric, dried fenugreek leaves, the remaining 1 teaspoon of chili powder, and remaining 1 teaspoon of salt. Stir together, add the kofta to the cooker, and toss to coat with the sauce for a few minutes.

6. If you like a gravy, add enough hot water so the kofta are half covered. If you prefer a thicker sauce, use less water.

7. Cover and cook for 4 hours on low, or for 2 to 3 hours on high. If you want to leave it to cook for longer, that's fine, too.

8. Throw in the garam masala and coriander leaves just before serving.

TECHNIQUE TIP: To save time, you can make the kofta the night before and keep them covered in the refrigerator until you cook the dish. You could also freeze them raw to use another time. Make sure they are defrosted before cooking.

Slow-Cooked North Indian Lamb
Mughlai Gosht

SERVES 6 TO 8

PREP TIME: 10 MINUTES | COOK TIME: 7 HOURS ON LOW OR 5 HOURS ON HIGH

The Mughal Empire ruled India starting in the 1400s, giving rise to a cuisine that combined elements from Central Asia and North India, fused with Persian and Indian cuisines. The food was rich in spices, nuts, and dried fruits. Huge buffets would be prepared for emperors, consisting of only the finest ingredients. Pork and beef were avoided for cultural reasons, but goat, lamb, venison, and poultry were plentiful. The food was time-consuming to prepare and was all about indulgence, with meat on the bone braised low and slow to produce deep, rich sauces. Ground-spice meat was wrapped around swords and cooked over open coals to make delicious sheikh kebabs. This recipe is all about cooking gosht (lamb or mutton) low and slow without adding any water, to draw out the meat's amazing flavors—which perfectly combine with the aromatics of the spices to make an amazing dish.

3⅓ pounds (1½ kg) leg of lamb, on the bone, cut into bite-size pieces

7 garlic cloves, roughly chopped

2¾-inch (7-cm) piece fresh ginger, chopped

1 fresh green chile, roughly chopped, plus 2 fresh chiles, sliced lengthwise, optional

1½ teaspoons Kashmiri chili powder

2 tablespoons rapeseed oil

4 onions, thinly sliced

5 tomatoes, finely diced

1 teaspoon sea salt

2 to 3 tablespoons Greek yogurt

1 teaspoon gram flour

2 teaspoons coriander seeds, ground

1 teaspoon cumin seeds, ground

1 teaspoon turmeric

½ teaspoon freshly ground black pepper

Handful mint leaves, chopped

Handful fresh coriander leaves, chopped

½ teaspoon Garam Masala (page 23)

1. Put the lamb into a large mixing bowl. Crush the garlic, ginger, and green chile in a mortar and pestle. Sprinkle in the chili powder and smear over the lamb. Set aside to marinate for as long as you can leave it. (Overnight in the refrigerator is fine.)

2. When you are ready to cook, heat the slow cooker to high or sauté. Add the oil and the onions, then the marinated meat, and brown it for about 5 minutes, stirring occasionally.

3. Add the chopped tomatoes and cook so they begin to break down (2 to 3 minutes). Season with salt.

4. Cover and cook on high for 4 hours, or on low for 6 hours.

5. Mix the yogurt with the gram flour, coriander seeds, cumin seeds, turmeric, black pepper, mint, and coriander leaves (keep a few mint and coriander leaves for garnish). Add this mixture to the slow cooker one spoonful at a time, and stir to incorporate it fully. Cook another hour with the lid off.

6. Once cooked, add the garam masala, top with the 2 sliced chiles (if using) and the reserved mint and coriander leaves, and serve.

INGREDIENT TIP: The bone in a leg of lamb is very heavy, and you can't chop it at home. Look for bone-in lamb stew meat, or ask your butcher to chop the leg of lamb for you. If this isn't possible, you can use lamb shanks or shoulder chops.

Curried Pulled Lamb

Masala Gosht

 QUICK PREP | SERVES 6 TO 8

PREP TIME: 10 MINUTES | COOK TIME: 6 HOURS ON LOW OR 4 HOURS ON HIGH

I cook dishes like this for family parties all the time because they require very little preparation and the results are spectacular. You can save even more time by marinating the lamb overnight in the refrigerator. This is great when served in wraps, or with Plain Basmati Rice (page 180) or Whole-Wheat Flatbread (page 181). The fresh pomegranate gives a sweet-and-tart punch that is delicious with spiced lamb.

FOR THE MARINADE

About 4¼ pounds (2 kg) shoulder of lamb, trimmed

2 teaspoons cumin seeds

1 tablespoon coriander seeds

6 garlic cloves

1½-inch (4-cm) piece fresh ginger, peeled and roughly chopped

2 fresh green chiles, roughly chopped

1 teaspoon Kashmiri chili powder

Sea salt

1 teaspoon turmeric

FOR THE LAMB

2 tablespoons rapeseed oil

4 onions, sliced

2¾-inch (7-cm) piece cassia bark

6 green cardamom pods

2 bay leaves

1 tablespoon grated jaggery (or dark-brown sugar)

1 tablespoon malt vinegar

⅓ cup (100 mL) hot water

2 large tomatoes, roughly chopped

1 teaspoon sea salt

Handful fresh mint leaves, chopped

Handful fresh coriander leaves, chopped

1 fresh green chile, chopped

Seeds from 1 pomegranate

1 tablespoon Greek yogurt

TO MARINADE THE LAMB

1. Make sure the lamb fits in your slow cooker. If it doesn't, cut it into the largest possible pieces.

2. Grind the cumin and coriander seeds in your spice grinder. Make a spice paste by blending the garlic, ginger, chiles, and chili powder with the ground seeds in a food processor or blender. Add a little water and salt, and then purée until smooth. Stir in the turmeric.

3. Score the lamb with a sharp knife and rub half of the paste over the meat. Leave to marinate for as long as you can.

TO COOK THE LAMB

1. Heat the slow cooker to high or to sauté. Add the oil, and then add the onions, cassia bark, cardamom pods, and bay leaves. Cook for 5 to 6 minutes, stirring occasionally, until the onions are soft.

2. Add the jaggery and vinegar, and then stir in the remaining spice paste. Add the water to the bowl holding the spice paste and stir to deglaze the bowl and get the last bits. Add the water to the slow cooker. Cook for a few minutes, until the mixture in the cooker is aromatic. Then add the tomatoes and salt.

3. Put the lamb in the slow cooker and coat with the onion mixture. Cover and cook on low for 6 hours, or on high for 4 hours. The lamb should be tender and soft.

4. Using two large forks or spoons, lift the lamb out onto a cutting board and leave for a few minutes. Use two forks to gently shred the lamb. Place the meat on a wide platter.

5. Switch the cooker to high and thicken the sauce by reducing it for a few minutes, if necessary. Shoulder can be a very fatty cut, so you may need to skim off the fat from the sauce using a ladle. Remove the cassia bark, cardamom pods, and bay leaves, and then pour the thickened sauce over the shredded meat.

6. Top with the mint, coriander leaves, chopped chile, pomegranate seeds, and a drizzle of yogurt over the top.

INGREDIENT TIP: The best way to remove the pomegranate seeds is to slice the fruit in half along the equator. Hold it over a large bowl, cut-side down, and tap the outer skin with the back of a wooden spoon until the seeds pop out.

Kashmiri Lamb Stew

Lamb Rogan Josh

 QUICK PREP | **SERVES 6 TO 8**

PREP TIME: 10 MINUTES | **COOK TIME: 6¼ HOURS ON LOW OR 4¼ HOURS ON HIGH**

Rogan means "oil" in Farsi and "red" in Hindi, and *josh* means "passion" or "heat." Which tells you this dish is all about cooking in a red oil-based sauce with an intense heat. The color comes from a neutrally flavored spice known as ratanjot (or alkanet root), giving the dish its wonderful deep-red color. It can be difficult to come by, so I substitute it with Kashmiri chili powder here. The fennel and ginger add complex undertones, which come together with the creamy yogurt, to create a powerful, satisfying sauce. The dish has evolved over the years with the addition of onions and tomatoes—but for me, I like the simple approach, so I stick to the Kashmiri cooking style.

2 tablespoons mustard oil

Large pinch asafetida

1 teaspoon cumin seeds

2¾-inch (7-cm) piece cassia bark

3 cloves

2 dried Kashmiri chiles

2 black cardamom pods

2 green cardamom pods

1 teaspoon salt

1¾ pounds (800 g) boneless leg of lamb, cut into large chunks

1 teaspoon red Kashmiri chili powder

1 teaspoon hot chili powder (optional)

1 teaspoon ground ginger

1 teaspoon ground fennel seeds

About ¼ cup (50 mL) hot water

3 heaped tablespoons Greek yogurt

1 teaspoon Garam Masala (page 23)

1. Heat the slow cooker to high or use the sauté function. Add the mustard oil and heat to the smoking point. Turn the cooker off and let the oil cool down.

2. Reheat the slow cooker to high and add the asafetida. Then add the cumin seeds, cassia bark, cloves, whole chiles, black and green cardamom pods, and salt.

3. When the spices become fragrant, add the meat and stir to sear the meat for a few minutes.

4. Add the chili powders and let the meat cook for a few minutes. Then stir in the ginger and fennel seeds. Mix well.

5. Cover and cook on low for 6 hours, or on high for 4 hours. Check halfway through cooking and, if required, add some hot water.

6. When the meat is tender, stir in the yogurt, 1 tablespoon at a time, so it's fully incorporated, creating a silky sauce. Cook for about 15 minutes longer.

7. Add the garam masala. Check the seasoning and serve.

INGREDIENT TIP: Bringing mustard oil to smoking point is a classic Indian technique for ridding the oil of any impurities. If you do not have mustard oil, just use rapeseed oil and skip the first step.

Slow-Cooked Lamb Shanks

Hyderabadi Shanks

SERVES 6 TO 8

PREP TIME: 20 MINUTES | COOK TIME: 8 HOURS ON LOW OR 6 HOURS ON HIGH

Hyderabadi cuisine is the native style of cooking for Muslims from the state of Hyderabad. It originated in the royal courts of the Nizam rulers, who came to power in the 1700s. The cuisine is an amalgamation of Turkish, Arabic, and Persian influences, along with some South Indian flavors. Hyderabad has a rich history of pearl and diamond trading, and legend has it that they would crush pearls into dishes and have banquets with hundreds of such extravagantly prepared foods. It's a meat-heavy cuisine and is known to use lots of offal, including tongue and brain.

6 lamb shanks

4 tablespoons vegetable oil

2¾-inch (7-cm) piece cassia bark

5 green cardamom pods

6 cloves

4 onions, peeled and thinly sliced

2-inch (5-cm) piece fresh ginger

5 garlic cloves

3 fresh green chiles, chopped

1 teaspoon turmeric

1 to 2 teaspoons Kashmiri chili powder

1 teaspoon ground cumin

1 tablespoon coriander seeds, ground

Sea salt

4 tomatoes, chopped

1 cup (250 mL) hot water

½ tablespoon Garam Masala (page 23)

Handful fresh coriander leaves

Julienned fresh ginger, for garnish

1. Make sure the shanks fit into the slow cooker.

2. Heat the cooker to high and add the oil. Brown the shanks one at a time. Remove the shanks and set aside.

3. Add the cassia bark, green cardamom pods, and cloves to the oil in the slow cooker. When fragrant, add the sliced onions and cook until they are golden, about 6 to 7 minutes.

4. Crush the ginger and garlic in a mortar and pestle and add to the cooker, along with the green chiles. Stir and add the turmeric, chili powder, cumin, coriander seeds, and season with salt.

5. Add the chopped tomatoes and stir. Then add the shanks back into the cooker and coat with the masala. Pour in the water to add some moisture.

6. Cover and cook on low for 8 hours, or on high for 6 hours, until the lamb is soft and coming away from the bone. Check the seasoning and adjust if required.

7. Remove the shanks and the cassia bark. Add the garam masala to the sauce and, using an immersion or regular blender, purée the sauce so it's smooth and silky. Pour over the shanks. Top with coriander leaves and some julienned ginger to serve.

EASY ADJUSTMENT: For a creamier result, add a few tablespoons of yogurt to the sauce at the end.

Hot-and-Sour Lamb Parsi Stew

Lamb Dhansak

SERVES 6 TO 8

PREP TIME: 15 MINUTES | COOK TIME: 6 HOURS ON LOW OR 4 HOURS ON HIGH

The Parsi community came to India from Persia around the eighth century, bringing with them a wonderful culinary tradition. This classic slow-cooked Parsi dish is a rustic one-pot lamb, dhal, and vegetable stew. *Dhan* means "grain" or "dhal," and *sak* means "to stew." The tang from the tamarind, heat from the chiles, and sweetness from the vegetables all come together to create an exquisite balance of flavors.

½ cup split yellow chickpeas (toor dhal)

½ cup red lentils (masoor dhal)

½ cup split black lentils (urid dhal)

1 teaspoon cumin seeds

1 teaspoon coriander seeds

1½-inch (4-cm) piece cassia bark

4 green cardamom pods

4 black peppercorns

1 tablespoon dried fenugreek leaves

1 star anise

6 garlic cloves

1-inch (3-cm) piece fresh ginger

2 fresh green chiles

2 pounds (1 kg) leg of lamb, trimmed and cut into large chunks

2 tablespoons rapeseed oil

2 medium onions, diced

3 tomatoes, diced

1 teaspoon salt

1 teaspoon turmeric

1 eggplant, chopped into large chunks

½ pound (200 g) pumpkin, peeled, seeded, and chopped into large chunks

1 medium onion, cut into chunks

15 fresh mint leaves, chopped

1¾ cups (400 mL) hot water

1 tablespoon tamarind paste

Handful fresh coriander leaves, chopped

1. Wash all the dhal in a few changes of water.

2. In a dry frying pan, toast the cumin seeds, coriander seeds, cassia bark, cardamom pods, peppercorns, dried fenugreek leaves, and anise for a few moments until fragrant. Grind them all to a powder in a spice grinder.

3. In a mortar and pestle, blender, or spice grinder, grind the garlic, ginger, and green chiles to a paste. Mix with the ground spices.

4. Put the lamb in a large bowl and coat with the spice paste.

5. Heat the slow cooker to high, or to sauté if you have that function. Add the oil and diced onions and cook for a few minutes, until the onions start to brown.

6. Add the meat to brown it for a minute or two. Add the tomatoes, stir, and then add the salt, turmeric, eggplant, pumpkin, onion chunks, mint, and all of the dhal. Pour in the water. Cover and cook on low for 6 hours, or on high for 4 hours.

7. Check that the dhal are cooked through. Then add the tamarind paste. Switch the cooker to high, remove the cover, and reduce the sauce for 10 minutes.

8. Check the seasoning, add the coriander leaves, and serve.

SUBSTITUTION TIP: Instead of pumpkin, you could use butternut or kabocha squash, or sweet potato.

Mutton Cooked with Spices and Ground Lamb

Mutton Rara

SERVES 6 TO 8

PREP TIME: 15 MINUTES | COOK TIME: 8 HOURS ON LOW OR 6 HOURS ON HIGH

Cooked with a delightful concoction of whole spices, this dish is pungent and fragrant. Prepared very much in the North Indian–style with onions, ginger, and garlic, the flavorful ingredients are left to bubble away for a long time until the mutton produces a luscious, meaty gravy—made perfect in the slow cooker. Serve with some Whole-Wheat Flatbread (page 181).

3 teaspoons rapeseed oil

2¾-inch (7-cm) piece cassia bark

2 black cardamom pods

6 green cardamom pods

10 black peppercorns

4 cloves

2 star anise

2 bay leaves

1 teaspoon cumin seeds

4 onions, finely chopped

8 garlic cloves, minced

8 dried red Kashmiri chiles

4 to 5 tomatoes, finely chopped

1 tablespoon freshly grated ginger

1 teaspoon turmeric

2 teaspoons coriander seeds, ground

1 teaspoon sea salt

14 ounces (400 g) ground mutton or lamb

1¾ pounds (800 g) mutton or lamb chunks (preferably on the bone)

1 teaspoon Garam Masala (page 23)

Handful fresh coriander leaves, chopped

1. Heat the oil in a frying pan (or in the slow cooker if you have a sear setting). Toast the cassia bark, black and green cardamom pods, peppercorns, cloves, star anise, bay leaves, and cumin seeds until fragrant, about 1 minute. Add the onions and garlic and cook for about 5 to 10 minutes, until soft and just starting to brown.

2. While the onions are cooking, soak the chiles in some boiling water to let them soften (just a few minutes). Drain.

3. Add the tomatoes, ginger, turmeric, ground coriander seeds, salt, and soaked chiles to the slow cooker.

4. Add the ground lamb and, using a wooden spoon, break it up and coat with the sauce.

5. Stir in the pieces of mutton and give it all a good mix, so the meat begins to heat through.

6. Cover and cook on low for 8 hours, or on high for 6 hours.

7. When the meat is tender and cooked through, turn the slow cooker to sauté or high and take the lid off so the sauce reduces and thickens. If you feel there is residual oil from the meat, you can use a ladle and skim it off first. Cook for about 5 to 6 minutes more.

8. Turn the cooker off and stir in the garam masala. Then check the seasoning and adjust if necessary.

9. Garnish with coriander leaves and serve hot.

INGREDIENT TIP: Mutton is the meat from a mature sheep. And sticking strictly with the definition, the animal should be over two years old and the meat aged for at least two weeks. This gives a really well-flavored meat that is tender and juicy when cooked correctly. It's a cheap cut and can be ordered from your butcher.

Minced Lamb with Peas and Mushrooms

Keema

SERVES 6 TO 8

PREP TIME: 20 MINUTES | COOK TIME: 6 HOURS ON LOW OR 4 HOURS ON HIGH

Keema is always made with fresh sweet green peas and sometimes potatoes can be added, but I prefer my keema with peas and delicious chunks of mushrooms. There is no sauce as such; instead, the meat is beautifully flavored and left moist and succulent when cooked in the slow cooker. Simple and satisfying—a perfect midweek meal.

1 tablespoon vegetable oil

2 bay leaves

2 onions, finely chopped

5 garlic cloves, finely chopped

10 to 15 mushrooms, quartered

1 (14-ounce/400-g) can tomatoes

1 tablespoon freshly grated ginger

1 teaspoon salt

1 teaspoon turmeric

2 teaspoons ground cumin

1 teaspoon chili powder

2 to 3 fresh green chiles, finely chopped

2 pounds (1 kg) lean ground lamb

1⅓ cups frozen peas, defrosted

2 teaspoons Garam Masala (page 23)

Handful fresh coriander leaves, chopped

1. Heat the oil in a frying pan (or in the slow cooker if you have a sear setting). When hot, add the bay leaves, then the onions and garlic. Cook for 5 to 10 minutes, until the onions start to cook through.

2. Add the mushrooms and stir for 1 to 2 minutes.

3. In the blender, blend the tomatoes to a purée. Add them to the pan, along with the ginger, salt, turmeric, cumin seeds, chili powder, and chiles, and stir.

4. Add the lamb and break it up with a wooden spoon. Mix thoroughly with the sauce. Cover and cook on low for 6 hours, or on high for 4 hours.

5. When cooked, add the peas and stir. Cook on high with the lid off until the peas are cooked and any liquid has evaporated, about 5 to 10 minutes. Stir occasionally. (This is an important step to ensure the dish is dry and delicious.)

6. Add the garam masala and fresh coriander to finish. Check the seasoning and serve.

SUBSTITUTION TIP: Ground beef, chicken, or turkey also work well. Just make sure the meat is lean, or the final dish may be a little oily.

South Indian Coconut-Pork Curry

Keralan Pandi

SERVES 6 TO 8

PREP TIME: 15 MINUTES | COOK TIME: 6 HOURS ON LOW OR 4 HOURS ON HIGH

Pork is a wonderful meat to use with the bold aromatic spicing of South India cuisine. The tougher cuts such as shoulder are transformed in the slow cooker and become marvelously tender and flavorsome. This is a wonderful dish using black pepper, star anise, and coconut milk and for a fresh twist I add a few colorful vegetables such as baby corn and green beans. Serve it simply with some fragrant Plain Basmati Rice (page 180).

2 pounds (1 kg) boneless pork shoulder, skin removed, cut into chunks

Sea salt

Freshly ground black pepper

2 tablespoons rapeseed oil

2 teaspoons cumin seeds

1 teaspoon coriander seeds

2 onions, finely diced

5 garlic cloves, minced

1 fresh green chile, chopped

1 tablespoon freshly grated ginger

1 teaspoon ground turmeric

2 star anise

2 dried red chiles

7 to 8 ounces (200 g) canned tomatoes

1 (14-ounce/400-g) can coconut milk

¼ pound (100 g) green beans, trimmed

Handful fresh coriander leaves, chopped

1. Season the pork with salt and lots of black pepper.

2. Heat the slow cooker to high, or to the sauté setting if you have one. Add the oil, and then add the pork to sear it for a minute or two.

3. Grind the cumin and coriander seeds in a mortar and pestle.

4. Add the onions, garlic, green chile, ginger, turmeric, anise, and red chiles to the ground cumin and coriander, and stir through.

5. Blend the tomatoes in the blender, and pour them into the slow cooker with the coconut milk. Cover and cook on low for 6 hours, or on high for 4 hours.

6. Half an hour before the end of cooking, add the trimmed beans and cook for 30 minutes more.

7. When cooked through, check the seasoning and add the coriander leaves.

EASY ADJUSTMENT: For a tangy twist, add 1 tablespoon of tamarind paste along with the coconut milk.

Pork Vindaloo

Vindaloo

SERVES 6 TO 8

**PREP TIME: 15 MINUTES, PLUS TIME TO MARINATE | COOK TIME: 6 ½ HOURS ON LOW
OR 4 ½ HOURS ON HIGH**

This Portuguese stew is a telling example of India's history: The Portuguese colonized Goa for more than 300 years, bringing with them chiles and wine. Vindaloo is an evolution of a pork stew called *carne de vinha d'alhos*, which was made with pork and garlic. Over time, the wine was swapped out for a local vinegar, while added were spices and chiles—and so the vindaloo became an Indian dish.

1 teaspoon cumin seeds

2 teaspoons coriander seeds

4 cloves

6 to 8 dried Kashmiri chiles

1 teaspoon black peppercorns

2 teaspoons mustard seeds, divided

2 onions, roughly chopped

6 garlic cloves

1-inch (3-cm) piece fresh ginger

4 to 5 tablespoons malt vinegar

3⅓ pounds (1½ kg) lean pork shoulder, skin removed, cut into chunks

1 teaspoon turmeric

1 teaspoon salt

1 tablespoon vegetable oil

½ to 1 teaspoon dark-brown sugar

1. In your spice grinder, grind the cumin seeds, coriander seeds, cloves, chiles, peppercorns, and 1 teaspoon of mustard seeds to a fine powder.

2. Place the spices in a blender with the onions, garlic, ginger, vinegar, and a splash of water, and blend to make a paste.

3. Put the meat in a large bowl and sprinkle with the turmeric, salt, and 2 tablespoons of the spice paste. Mix with your hands so that all the meat is coated. Cover and leave for as long as you can (at least 20 minutes, or overnight, in the refrigerator).

4. Turn the slow cooker to high, or to sauté, and heat the oil. Add 1 teaspoon of the mustard seeds, and when they pop add the remaining spice paste and cook until fragrant, 1 to 2 minutes. Add the marinated meat, stir, and sear the meat for a few minutes.

5. Cover and cook on low for 6 hours, or on high for 4 hours.

6. When the meat is cooked through, stir in the sugar, cover, and cook for another 15 minutes.

7. Turn the cooker to high, remove the lid, and cook off any juices. The final dish should be delicious, with a thick sauce that just clings to the meat.

EASY ADJUSTMENT: Vindaloo does not have to be very hot! Just reduce the number of chiles. Or you can substitute some paprika to get the color without the heat. You can also reduce the amount of black pepper used. Serve it with a cooling Pomegranate Raita (page 172).

Slow-Cooked Indian-Spiced Brisket

Gosht Assado

 QUICK PREP | **SERVES 6 TO 8**

PREP TIME: 5 MINUTES | **COOK TIME: 8 HOURS ON LOW OR 6 HOURS ON HIGH**

Beef is eaten by Indian Muslim and Christian communities, and is popular in the South and in Bangladesh. This dish is essentially a South Indian pot roast—*assado* means "roast" in Portuguese. Brisket is tough, so low and slow is the key here, gradually producing a deliciously flavored beef dish that is succulent and super tender. Beef brisket nicely takes on the bold flavors of Indian spices, transforming the meat into something spectacular. Requiring very little preparation, this dish is accomplished by the slow cooker, which does all the work of penetrating the dish with irresistible flavor. Stuff the meat into Whole-Wheat Flatbread (page 181), Naan (page 184), or pita bread with fresh Spiced Mango Salsa (page 173) and enjoy.

2 tablespoons rapeseed oil

1 large onion, cut into rings

2 fresh red chiles, finely chopped

5 garlic cloves, puréed

1 tablespoon freshly grated ginger

1 tablespoon Garam Masala (page 23)

2 teaspoons turmeric

1 tablespoon ground cumin

1 tablespoon coriander seeds, ground

4 to 6 chopped tomatoes (14 ounces/400 g)

1 cup (250 mL) hot water

2 pounds (1 kg) beef brisket

1 bunch fresh coriander leaves, chopped

2 fresh red chiles sliced

4 scallions, sliced

1. Heat the slow cooker to high or sauté, and add the oil. Stir in the onions and cook until they soften. Then add the chile, garlic, and ginger, and stir.

2. Add the garam masala, turmeric, cumin seeds, coriander seeds, and tomatoes, and mix. Then pour in the water and add the beef brisket.

3. Cover and cook on low for 8 hours, or on high for 6 hours, until the meat is tender. Remove the meat from the pan and cover it with foil to keep warm.

4. Using an immersion or regular blender, purée the juices and either simmer them on high, uncovered in the slow cooker, or transfer to the stovetop to produce a glaze (about 5 minutes).

5. Pull the meat apart with two forks and place on a platter. Pour the glaze over the meat and mix through. Garnish with fresh coriander leaves, sliced chiles, and scallions.

EASY ADJUSTMENT: You can add 1 tablespoon of honey to the glaze to thicken it, which also adds a dash of sweetness.

Braised Tamarind Pork Ribs

Imli Pasiliyaan

SERVES 6 TO 8

PREP TIME: 20 MINUTES | COOK TIME: 8 HOURS ON LOW OR 6 HOURS ON HIGH

I love ribs—be they served as a snack or as a starter. And this dish makes excellent use of ribs, marinating them in classic Indian flavors like tamarind, fennel, and chiles. Thanks to the slow cooker, the meat gradually becomes tender and the spices have enough time to entwine with the marinade, making the whole thing lip-smacking delicious!

⅓ cup tamarind pulp

2¾ cups (650 mL) boiling water

8 garlic cloves, minced

1½-inch (4-cm) piece fresh ginger, grated

⅓ cup (100 mL) soy sauce

2 teaspoons coriander seeds, ground

2 star anise

1 teaspoon fennel seeds

2 fresh green chiles, finely chopped

⅓ cup dark-brown sugar

2 racks of pork ribs, 1¾ to 2 pounds (800 to 900 g)

1. Place the tamarind pulp in a bowl and add the boiling water. Let it soak for 15 minutes, and then mash it up using a fork. Strain the tamarind water into a large bowl and discard all the solids.

2. Preheat the slow cooker on high. Pour in the tamarind liquid, garlic, ginger, soy sauce, ground coriander seeds, anise, fennel seeds, chopped chiles, and brown sugar. Stir until all of the sugar dissolves.

3. Using a sharp knife, scrape the underside of the ribs on one end, and you will see a transparent membrane. Pull this membrane (use a cloth for a better grip) from the back of the ribs to remove it. If the full rack doesn't fit into the cooker, cut it into smaller racks.

4. Put the ribs into the cooker and make sure they are submerged in the marinade. Cover and cook on low for 8 hours, or on high for 6 hours.

5. When cooked, remove the ribs and either cover them in foil to keep warm, or finish them in the oven for 20 minutes at 350°F (180°C) to crisp them up.

6. Turn the slow cooker to high, remove the cover, and reduce the sauce to thicken, about 5 minutes. Push through a sieve and use as a dipping sauce or drizzle over the cooked ribs.

EASY ADJUSTMENT: For extra heat, sprinkle some dried red chili flakes on the ribs after they are cooked.

Creamy Rice Pudding *page 153*

Chapter Nine

Sweets and Desserts

Sweet Condensed Milk

Rabri

CONTAINS NUTS ● QUICK PREP ● VEGETARIAN | SERVES 6 TO 8
PREP TIME: 10 MINUTES | COOK TIME: 6 HOURS (3 HOURS ON HIGH, THEN 3 HOURS ON LOW)

Rabri is a very popular North Indian dish, usually made by reducing milk on the stovetop until the liquid is thick and sweet. The layers of cream rise to the surface, from where they are collected and served in the reduced milk, which is flavored with saffron. For a similar consistency in the slow cooker, I use ricotta cheese.

4 cups (1 liter) heavy cream

4 cups (1 liter) whole milk, plus 5 tablespoons, optional

15 ounces (425 g) full-fat ricotta cheese

3 tablespoons crushed mixed unsalted nuts (almonds, cashews, pistachios)

1 teaspoon saffron (optional)

2 teaspoons ground cardamom

1 cup sugar

1. Mix the heavy cream, whole milk, and ricotta cheese in the slow cooker. Cover and cook on high for 3 hours.

2. Soak the saffron in the milk for 20 minutes, just before you're ready to add it.

3. Add the nuts, saffron, and additional milk (if using), and cardamom powder. Cover and cook on low for another 2 hours.

4. Add the sugar and cook for another 1 hour on low. You may need to scrape the sides down a few times.

5. Turn the cooker off and refrigerate the rabri. Serve cold.

EASY ADJUSTMENT: If you prefer your desserts less sweet, just reduce the amount of sugar. And for a more exotic fragrance, swap the cardamom powder for a teaspoon of rose water.

Creamy Rice Pudding

Kheer

CONTAINS NUTS ⚬ QUICK PREP ⚬ VEGETARIAN | SERVES 6 TO 8
PREP TIME: 5 MINUTES | COOK TIME: 3 HOURS ON HIGH

Kheer is a classic Indian pudding that is all about comfort and homeyness. My simple slow-cooker version is thick, creamy, and delicious. If you want to jazz it up, try serving it with a mixed berry or mango compote, or just stick to the traditional way of serving it with nuts and raisins.

1 teaspoon butter or ghee

½ cup basmati rice, washed and drained

2 tablespoons sugar

½ teaspoon green cardamom seeds, lightly crushed

2 green cardamom pods

2 tablespoons golden raisins (optional)

5 cups (1¼ liters) whole milk

2 tablespoons crushed unsalted pistachios

1. Coat the bottom and sides of your slow cooker with the butter or ghee.

2. Put the rice, sugar, cardamom seeds, cardamom pods, raisins, and milk in the slow cooker.

3. Cover and cook on high for 3 hours, stirring once or twice during cooking.

4. You can serve this hot or cold. It will thicken as it cools. Sprinkle with chopped nuts just before serving.

TECHNIQUE TIP: If your kheer hasn't thickened enough by the end of the cooking time, you can take the lid off and cook for a little while longer, until you are happy with the consistency.

Pakistani Sweet Rice Scented with Cardamom

Zarda

◯ CONTAINS NUTS ✳ QUICK PREP ◔ VEGETARIAN | SERVES 6 TO 8
PREP TIME: 10 MINUTES | COOK TIME: 2 HOURS ON HIGH AND 15 MINUTES ON LOW

This beautiful golden sweet-rice dish is served up for all special occasions—from weddings to religious ceremonies. It's an easy dessert to cook for lots of people, and the slow cooker makes that process even simpler.

2 cups basmati rice

4 tablespoons butter or ghee

4 cups (1 liter) hot water

1 large pinch saffron, crushed and mixed with 2 tablespoons hot water, or a yellow food coloring

6 green cardamom pods

¾ to 1 cup sugar

2 tablespoons crushed unsalted pistachios

2 tablespoons slivered almonds

1. Wash the rice in a few changes of water until it runs clear, and then soak it in warm water for 10 minutes.

2. Rub a little of the butter or ghee on the inside of your slow cooker and turn it to high. Drain the washed rice and place it in the slow cooker. Add the hot water and saffron water (or the food coloring). Stir to mix. This should color the rice, giving it the bright yellow it's famous for.

3. Cover and cook for 2 hours on high. Stir the rice halfway through the cooking time. When cooked, remove the rice and set it aside in a colander.

4. Turn the cooker to high and add the rest of the butter to melt, then crack in the cardamom pods. Stir in the sugar and 4 tablespoons of water (add a little more if required). Stir to melt the sugar.

5. Cook gently for about 5 minutes to produce a syrup. Add most of the nuts, reserving some for a garnish.

6. Gently stir the rice back into the cooker and fold it, so that each grain is coated with the sugar syrup.

7. Cover and turn the cooker to low. Cook for another 5 to 10 minutes.

8. Serve warm, topped with the remaining nuts.

EASY ADJUSTMENT: You can also add a few tablespoons of golden raisins when you make the sugar syrup—but I'm not a raisin fan, so I leave them out.

Sweet Rice and Almond Porridge

Phirni

CONTAINS NUTS ● QUICK PREP ● VEGETARIAN | SERVES 6 TO 8
PREP TIME: 10 MINUTES | COOK TIME: 6 HOURS (4 HOURS ON HIGH AND 2 HOURS ON LOW)

I first tried phirni in a famous dhabba, or food shack, called Kesar da Dhaba, which was established in 1916 in Amritsar, the capital city of Punjab that is holy to the Sikh religion. It was served in little individual clay pots set on an ice tray, and I immediately fell in love with it. Different from kheer, it's cooked with a rice-and-nut paste.

⅓ cup basmati rice

⅓ cup almonds

4 cups (1 liter) whole milk, divided

¾ cup sugar

Generous pinch saffron strands (optional)

6 green cardamom pods, seeds only, pounded to a fine powder

Handful of crushed unsalted pistachios, for garnish

1. Wash the rice and soak it in water for 30 minutes.

2. In a blender, grind the rice and almonds with about ⅔ cup (150 mL) of the milk to a coarse paste.

3. Add the remaining milk and blend to a smooth paste.

4. Pour the mixture into your slow cooker. Cover and cook on high for 4 hours.

5. Add the sugar, saffron (if using), and pounded cardamom seeds. Cover and cook on low for 2 more hours.

6. Transfer into individual ceramic dishes or a large clay or earthenware pot, and leave to cool for 4 to 5 hours.

7. Garnish with pistachios and serve chilled.

INGREDIENT TIP: If you want to go fully authentic, phirni is always served with a flurry of edible silver leaves on top. You can buy them at Indian grocery stores and online.

Steamed Yogurt Pudding

Bhapi Doi

⊛ QUICK PREP ◐ VEGETARIAN | SERVES 6 TO 8
PREP TIME: 5 MINUTES | COOK TIME: 4 HOURS ON LOW

This is a light, steamed pudding that can be flavored with almost anything you like, from cinnamon to vanilla to rose water. In fact, this recipe offers all three options, but you should pick just one—the three don't work well together. This dish has the consistency of panna cotta, and can be served in many different ways. For example, I enjoy it topped with a mixed-berry reduction. This pudding really needs to be cooked on low to ensure the yogurt sets perfectly.

7 to 8 ounces (200 g) condensed milk

1 cup (200 g) full-fat yogurt

7 to 8 ounces (200 g) light cream or half-and-half

Seeds from 1 vanilla pod or 1 teaspoon pure vanilla extract OR

1 teaspoon rose water OR

½ teaspoon cinnamon

1. In a large pitcher, mix the condensed milk, yogurt, cream, and vanilla (or rose water, or cinnamon—depending on which flavoring you are using).

2. Pour the cream mixture into a heat-proof ceramic dish with a lid, or into individual pots with lids.

3. Place a rack or scrunched-up foil in the bottom of your slow cooker so that the dish or pots can rest on it. Turn the slow cooker to high and pour in about 1 cup (250 mL) of hot water.

4. Cover the filled dish or pots and place in the slow cooker. Cover the slow cooker and cook on low for 4 hours.

5. The pudding should set with a little wobble. When cooked, remove the dessert from the slow cooker and immediately take off any lids, so the pudding cools. Place in the refrigerator until you're ready to eat.

TECHNIQUE TIP: You must cook this dessert in a covered container because it needs to steam. But once cooked, immediately remove the lid to let the dessert cool and to prevent any condensation from dripping inside.

Stewed Apricots

Khubani ka Meeta

CONTAINS NUTS QUICK PREP VEGETARIAN | SERVES 6 TO 8
PREP TIME: 10 MINUTES | COOK TIME: 4 HOURS ON LOW OR 2 HOURS ON HIGH

The name of this dish from the Hyderabad region translates to "apricot sweet." It's a simple stewed fruit dessert that is warming and foolproof to make, especially in the slow cooker. And because you use dried fruit, you can make it even when apricots are not in season. You can also experiment with other dried fruits—mangos and apples are both great. It's delicious served with the Homemade Greek-Style Yogurt (page 176), and it even makes an excellent oatmeal topping. Leave off the toppers, and you have yourself a vegan- and nut-free dessert.

1⅓ pounds (600 g) dried apricots, pitted

1 teaspoon ground cinnamon

1 cup granulated sugar

1 to 1¼ cups (200 to 300 mL) water

⅓ cup (100 mL) heavy cream

2 tablespoons toasted almond slivers

1. Turn the slow cooker to high and add the apricots, cinnamon, sugar, and water.

2. Cover and cook on high for 2 hours, or on low for 4 hours.

3. Leave to cool in a large bowl, then chill in the refrigerator.

4. Just before you're ready to serve, whip the cream. Serve chilled in individual glasses, topped with whipped cream and nuts.

EASY ADJUSTMENT: If you feel the dish is too wet, cook it on high with the lid off for a few more minutes, this will surely reduce the excess liquid.

Sweet Carrot Stew

Gajrela ka Halwa

CONTAINS NUTS ⦿ QUICK PREP ◐ VEGETARIAN | SERVES 6 TO 8

PREP TIME: 10 MINUTES | COOK TIME: 6 HOURS ON HIGH

Halwa is a sweet that can be made with many different vegetables, from pumpkin to carrots to zucchini. This one is made with carrots, and is the most popular halwa dish across India. The carrots are cooked low and slow in milk, until they are soft and tender. These Indian desserts can be very sweet, so you can certainly reduce the amount of sugar to suit your taste.

2 pounds (1 kg) carrots, peeled

4 cups (1 liter) whole milk

2 cups sugar, plus 1 tablespoon

6 green cardamom pods, crushed

⅔ cup raisins

3 tablespoons ghee or butter

2 tablespoons almond slivers

1. Grate the carrots and put them in the slow cooker with the milk. Cover and cook for 4 hours on high.

2. Add the 2 cups sugar, cardamom pods, and raisins. Stir, cover, and cook for another 2 hours on high.

3. Remove the lid, add the ghee or butter, almonds, and 1 tablespoon sugar, and stir on high, or change the setting to sauté, and stir until the stew dries out and becomes glossy (about 5 minutes).

- -

TECHNIQUE TIP: Rather than cooking in two stages, you can just put everything into the pot and cook on high for 6 to 8 hours—just know that the carrots will not break down completely and you will not get the glossy finish so characteristic of authentic halwa.

Steamed Cucumber Cake

Tavsali or Dhondas

CONTAINS NUTS | VEGAN | SERVES 6 TO 8
PREP TIME: 15 MINUTES | COOK TIME: 2 TO 3 HOURS ON HIGH

I know, cucumber cake sounds unusual—but this Goan-style steamed cake is a perfect dessert for the slow cooker. The traditional version uses a yellow cucumber, which is a bigger and fleshier cucumber, but the recipe works just as well with an ordinary green cucumber. The batter needs to be thick, like a goopy pancake batter, so be mindful you don't make it too wet. If it comes out too thick, you can add a little milk to thin it out. And remember, it will have a different texture than a baked cake—and will surprise you with a wonderfully refreshing flavor of cucumber.

2 cups semolina flour

1½ pounds (700 g) cucumbers

½ teaspoon coconut oil

1 teaspoon baking powder, plus more for dusting

1½ cups grated jaggery (or dark-brown sugar)

2 cups freshly grated coconut

6 green cardamom pods, seeds only, pounded

3 tablespoons cashews, roughly crushed

Pinch salt

½ teaspoon baking soda

1. Preheat the slow cooker on high.

2. In a large, dry frying pan, roast the semolina flour over low heat for 3 to 4 minutes, until it becomes aromatic. Remove from the pan and set aside.

3. Peel and grate the cucumbers into a large bowl.

4. Grease a pan (one that will fit inside your slow cooker) with the coconut oil and dust it with a pinch of baking powder. Set aside.

5. In a large bowl, mix the cucumber (with all its water), roasted semolina, jaggery, coconut, cardamom seeds, cashews, and salt into a batter. Add the baking powder and baking soda, and mix well.

6. Pour into the prepared cake pan. Cover the outside of the pan with foil.

7. Set a rack inside the slow cooker, or put some scrunched-up foil on the bottom. Pour in about 1 to 1¼ cups (250 to 300 mL) hot water and place the pan inside the cooker. Cover and cook on high for 2 to 3 hours.

8. Check if the cake is cooked by putting the tip of a knife into it. If it comes out clean, it's ready.

9. Leave to cool before removing the cake from the pan.

TECHNIQUE TIP: It can be a little tricky to get the cake out of the pan—be patient! And you may need to use a knife to scrape around the sides. A springform pan may be a better option.

Chocolate-Chile Cheesecake

Chokalat Mitee Malai

 VEGETARIAN | SERVES 8 TO 10

PREP TIME: 15 MINUTES | COOK TIME: 2½ HOURS ON HIGH, PLUS 1 HOUR TO SET

This is not actually an Indian recipe, but I'm a bit of a chocolate fan, and I love cheesecake, so including this delicacy was a no-brainer for me. I always add a little chile, which in my mind gives the cheesecake that Indian twist. When melting the chocolate, remember to make sure the simmering water does not touch the bottom of the glass bowl. Cheesecake is the perfect dessert for the slow cooker, so do give this recipe a try. And I hope you love this one as much as I do.

FOR THE CRUST

3 cups chocolate digestive biscuits (or chocolate graham crackers, or any plain chocolate cookies), crushed

1 tablespoon unsweetened cocoa powder

⅔ cup unsalted butter, melted

FOR THE FILLING

1 pound (500 g) cream cheese

⅔ cup (150 mL) sour cream

3 large eggs, plus 3 egg yolks

¾ cup sugar

5 to 6 ounces (175 g) dark chocolate (you can use chili chocolate)

½ tablespoon unsweetened cocoa powder mixed with 1 tablespoon hot water

3 to 4 dried chiles, very finely crushed

TO MAKE THE CRUST

1. Place a rack in the bottom of the slow cooker, or scrunch up foil to create a zigzag across the bottom of the cooker so a cake pan can sit on top of it. Add about 1 cup (250 mL) of hot water.

2. Grease a 7-inch springform pan.

3. Mix the crushed biscuits, cocoa, and melted butter, and press the mixture into the bottom of the springform pan. Even the layer out and put it into the freezer for about 10 minutes.

TO MAKE THE FILLING

1. In a large bowl, beat the cream cheese to soften. Then add the sour cream, followed by the eggs and egg yolks. Beat in the sugar until it's all mixed together.

2. Simmer some water in a pan and place the chocolate into a glass bowl that will sit over the pan but not touch the water. Melt the chocolate gently and set aside. (You can also put the chocolate in a bowl and melt it in the microwave for 1 minute on high. Stir to ensure it has melted through.)

3. In a smaller bowl, combine the melted chocolate and the cocoa-and-water mixture, and then add the crushed chiles and mix well. Add the chile mixture to the cream mixture and mix completely so it's smooth.

4. Take the crust out of the freezer, and line the outside of the springform with foil. Pour the chocolate filling into the pan.

5. Place it gently onto the rack or foil in the slow cooker, so it's not touching the sides.

6. Switch the slow cooker to high and put a kitchen towel over the top of the cooker. Place the lid on top of the towel and cook on high for 2½ hours.

7. Turn the cooker off, don't open it, and leave the cake to sit for another hour inside the cooker.

8. After an hour, remove the pan from the slow cooker, take the foil off, and allow it to cool completely before refrigerating overnight.

9. To serve, let the cake stand at room temperature for about 20 minutes before removing it from the pan. Serve with a big dollop of whipped cream and enjoy!

- -

PORTION TIP: To make a smaller cheesecake, just halve the ingredients and cook everything in a 5-inch pan for the same amount of time.

(Left to right) Red Pepper and Tomato Chutney page 169, Spiced Mango Salsa page 173, and Mint Chutney *page 170*

Chapter Ten

Chutneys
and Staples

Tamarind and Ginger Chutney
Saunth ki Chutney

(V) VEGAN | MAKES 3 TO 4 CUPS

PREP TIME: 15 MINUTES | COOK TIME: 4 HOURS ON LOW

This is a perfect chutney to serve up with starters, because it incorporates everything that is so essential about an Indian condiment: heat, tang, sweetness, and spice—what we collectively call chaat patta. This chutney is usually served with starters—such as samosas and pakora—and would also be used with the Spicy Pulled Chicken (page 108).

4 cups (1 liter) hot water

1 pound (500 g) seedless tamarind pulp

1 pound (500 g) grated jaggery (or dark-brown sugar)

2 teaspoons kala namak (pink salt) or 1 teaspoon Chaat Masala (page 23)

2 teaspoons Garam Masala (page 23)

2 teaspoons ground ginger

2 teaspoons chili powder, or to taste

1 teaspoon freshly ground black pepper

1 teaspoon salt

1. Preheat the slow cooker on high and place all of the ingredients into it. Cover and cook for 4 hours on low. Give it a stir halfway through the cooking, if you can.

2. For the last hour, remove the lid to help the chutney reduce a little.

3. Turn the cooker off, scrape everything out, and strain through a sieve into a large bowl. Leave to cool.

4. When the chutney cools, pour it into a clean, sterilized jar, and keep it in the refrigerator for up to 3 weeks.

- -

INGREDIENT TIP: Different tamarinds can have different potencies, so taste yours to see how tangy it happens to be.

Date and Tamarind Chutney

Imli Chutney

⊛ QUICK PREP   Ⓥ VEGAN | MAKES 3 TO 4 CUPS

PREP TIME: 10 MINUTES | COOK TIME: 6 HOURS ON LOW

This chutney is made with tamarind for the tang, and the dates deliver a hit of sugar that makes the dessert really Moorish. It's easy to make in a slow cooker, and is great with so many different dishes—including Chickpea Curry (page 76) and Braised Tamarind Pork Ribs (page 148).

4 cups (1 liter) hot water

1 pound (500 g) seedless tamarind pulp

1 pound (500 g) seedless dates

1 pound (500 g) grated jaggery (or dark-brown sugar)

4 teaspoons kala namak (black salt) or 1 teaspoon Chaat Masala (page 23)

3 teaspoons chili powder

2 teaspoons cumin seeds, roasted and ground

2 teaspoons crushed black peppercorns

1 teaspoon coriander seeds, ground

1 teaspoon coarse-grain salt

1. Heat the slow cooker to high and place all of the ingredients inside. Cover and cook for 6 hours on low. Give it a stir halfway through the cooking, if you can.

2. For the last hour, remove the lid to help the chutney reduce a little.

3. Turn the cooker off, scrape everything out, and strain through a sieve into a large bowl. Leave to cool.

4. When the chutney cools, pour it into a clean, sterilized jar, and keep it in the refrigerator for up to 3 weeks.

INGREDIENT TIP: You can use tamarind paste instead of pulp, but you will need about 2 pounds (1 kg) and should add about ⅓ cup (100 mL) of water to dilute it before adding it to the cooker. Do not use a tamarind concentrate, as it doesn't have the best flavor, and it's very dark in color.

Indian Tomato Ketchup with Pickling Spices

Tamatar ki Chutney

⚜ QUICK PREP   Ⓥ VEGAN | MAKES 2 CUPS
PREP TIME: 10 MINUTES | COOK TIME: 2 HOURS ON LOW

This is a delicious sweet-and-spicy tomato chutney made with panch phoran, which gives it its dynamic flavor. I use this as a relish on burgers, as a dip with papadums (thin, crisp, fried breads), or on the side with curry dishes. Try it with the Hot Goan-Style Coconut Chicken (page 120).

1 to 1½ cups grated jaggery (or dark-brown sugar)

¾ cup (200 mL) white vinegar

3 tablespoons rapeseed oil

1 tablespoon Panch Phoran (page 23)

2 to 4 dried Kashmiri red chiles

2 pounds (1 kg) tomatoes, quartered

1 teaspoon salt

1 teaspoon chili powder (optional)

1. In a large bowl, mix the jaggery with the vinegar until it is dissolved.

2. Heat the slow cooker to high and add the oil. Add the panch phoran and cook until the spices sizzle and become fragrant. This should only take 1 minute. Add the dried chiles, and then pour the vinegar-and-sugar mixture into the cooker, and stir.

3. Add in the tomatoes and switch the cooker to low. Cover and cook for 2 hours on low.

4. Season with the salt and chili powder (if using), then stir. If you want to remove any of the tomato skins, do so with a pair of tongs.

5. Put the chutney into a sterilized glass jar and leave it to cool. When cooled, seal the jar. The chutney will keep for 4 to 6 weeks in the refrigerator.

- -

SIMPLE SUBSTITUTION: You can use canned tomatoes, but fresh ones give a brighter and more delicious flavor.

Red Pepper and Tomato Chutney

Kati Shimla Mirch ki Chutney

✳ QUICK PREP ⓥ VEGAN | MAKES 2 TO 3 CUPS
PREP TIME: 10 MINUTES | COOK TIME: 4 HOURS ON LOW

This chutney is bold and robust, and works with lots of veggie starters—it's even great as a dip for your chips. Simple to make in a slow cooker, you just chop the veggies, add everything into the cooker, and then blend it—simple! This chutney is really good with the Vegetable Korma with Almonds (page 94) for some added flavor.

3 tablespoons rapeseed oil

1 teaspoon cumin seeds

4 garlic cloves, roughly chopped

1 large red onion, roughly chopped

2 red bell peppers, seeded and roughly chopped

1 pound (500 g) fresh tomatoes

1 tablespoon malt vinegar

1 teaspoon salt

1 fresh green chile

¼ cup (50 mL) hot water

1. Heat the slow cooker to high and add the oil.

2. Add the cumin seeds and cook until they are fragrant. Then stir in the garlic and cook 1 to 2 minutes.

3. Add the onion, peppers, tomatoes, vinegar, salt, chile, and water.

4. Cook on low for 4 hours, until the peppers are soft and the tomatoes have burst.

5. Using an immersion or regular blender, purée, and then pour the chutney through a colander.

6. Put the chutney into a sterilized glass jar and leave to cool. When cooled, seal the jar. The chutney will keep for 2 weeks in the refrigerator.

EASY ADJUSTMENT: If you have an intolerance to tomatoes, a sauce based entirely on bell peppers is great for curries: Instead of the tomatoes, make a paste using 4 or 5 red, yellow, and orange peppers. Cook them down with about ⅓ cup of water, and then blend the mixture with an immersion blender. Add this paste instead of the tomato paste.

Mint Chutney

Pudina Chutney

⚙ QUICK PREP Ⓥ VEGAN | MAKES 1 CUP
PREP TIME: 10 MINUTES

This is the first thing my mum had me make on my own, from scratch—from sending me out to the garden to pick the fresh mint leaves, to pounding the mint and onions. I can still feel the tears running from my eyes as I was crushing the onions. This chutney takes only a few minutes to make—that's why there's no cooking time included—and it's so fresh and zingy that your whole mouth will be tingling with excitement. It's superb with the Chettinad Chicken (page 116) and the Whole Tandoori-Style Braised Chicken (page 112).

1 or 2 lemons

Large bunch fresh mint leaves

1 fresh green chile (add more for more heat)

1 onion, cut into chunks

1 teaspoon salt

1. Slice the lemons in half and cut off the rinds. Remove any seeds and chop the flesh into quarters.

2. Remove the leaves from the mint and discard the stalks. Remove the chile stem.

3. Place all of the ingredients in a blender and purée until you get a finely blended chutney.

Cheater's Mint Raita

Pudina Raita

⊛ QUICK PREP ◐ VEGETARIAN | SERVES 6 TO 8
PREP TIME: 5 TO 7 MINUTES

A raita is any yogurt-based side dish. It can be plain or flavored with spices, vegetables, or fruit. This one is a real restaurant special, a quick-and-easy mint-yogurt raita that takes seconds to make. Being more of a relish, this raita will be delicious with the Spicy Stuffed Peppers (page 98) or the Cumin-Spiced Chicken Wings (page 109). And it's also perfect as a sauce for samosas and as a relish for lamb kebabs. I call this my "cheater" recipe, because it uses a store-bought mint sauce—the kind you buy to put on roasted lamb.

⅓ cup (100 mL)
Greek yogurt
Splash of milk

1 tablespoon mint sauce
1 teaspoon Garam Masala
(page 23)

Fresh mint, for garnish

1. Put the yogurt into a large bowl, and add a splash of milk. Mix, and add more milk, if necessary, to create a runny consistency.

2. Stir in the mint sauce.

3. Stir in the garam masala.

4. Refrigerate until required. Garnish with a sprig of mint.

INGREDIENT TIP: Indian meals are incomplete without the cooling element of yogurt. You can just have plain yogurt, or create something more extravagant. There are so many different types of raita dishes, and you can flavor yogurt with pretty much anything. Some of the more usual raitas are made with mint, cucumber, or spices like cumin seeds.

Pomegranate Raita

Anaar Raita

⬤ QUICK PREP ⬤ VEGETARIAN | SERVES 6 TO 8
PREP TIME: 10 MINUTES

I like this raita because it's slightly different, thanks to the wonderful pomegranate fruit. The little gems pop in your mouth, releasing that lovely sweet-and-fruity twang. A perfect little side for spicy dishes, with the pomegranate seeds adding that cooling element and sweetness. Try it with the Pork Vindaloo (page 144) or the Slow-Cooked Lamb Shanks (page 136).

1 cup plain Greek yogurt

½ teaspoon cumin seeds

2 tablespoons pomegranate seeds

2 tablespoons grated cucumber

1 teaspoon grated jaggery (or dark-brown sugar)

½ teaspoon salt

1. Put the yogurt into a large bowl and beat it a little to aerate.

2. Toast the cumin seeds in a dry frying pan until fragrant, about 1 minute, and then add to the yogurt.

3. Mix in all of the other ingredients and stir through.

4. Refrigerate until required.

Spiced Mango Salsa
Aamb ka Kachumber

✳ QUICK PREP Ⓥ VEGAN | SERVES 6 TO 8
PREP TIME: 10 MINUTES

A kachumber is a fresh chopped salad. I love having a selection of little sides and salads with meals, and this one is a favorite of mine because it combines colors of the rainbow and heavenly flavors to match. From the lovely sweetness of the mango, to the warmth of the red chile, to the pepperiness of the nigella seeds, this salsa has summer written all over it. What's even better is that it takes just a few minutes to put together. I'm certain you'll add this one to your summer recipe collection.

1 red onion, very finely diced	½ fresh red chile, finely chopped	1 large, ripe mango, peeled, pitted, and cubed
Handful fresh coriander leaves, chopped	Juice of 1 lime	½ teaspoon nigella seeds

1. Place the chopped onion, coriander leaves, and chile in a large bowl.

2. Add the lime juice, mango cubes, and nigella seeds.

3. Let stand for 10 minutes so the flavors can blend. Stir before serving.

Basic Brown-Onion Masala

Daag Masala

(V) **VEGAN | MAKES 4 CUPS**

PREP TIME: 20 MINUTES | COOK TIME: 6½ HOURS ON LOW

This is my basic homemade brown-onion masala. It's thick and rich, and has a robust flavor that can be used to create beautifully fragrant meat dishes. The onions are very slowly cooked down to produce a deep and rich golden-brown mass, into which are added the tomatoes and spices. When cooked, the masala is a dark-brown gloopy mass of aromatics and flavor. This technique of slow cooking is used in North India (originally by the Sindhi community) as a way of infusing lots of flavor into thick sauces, and is also as an effective method for preserving foods. Most Indian dishes require a base masala such as this one. Making this base removes some of the initial steps required by many of the recipes in this book. It's perfect for making the Punjabi Red Kidney Bean Curry (page 81), Punjabi Chicken Curry (page 118), and Spiced Potatoes and Cauliflower (page 89), to name just a few.

2 tablespoons rapeseed oil

6 onions, finely diced

8 garlic cloves, finely chopped

1¾ pounds (800 g) canned plum tomatoes

3-inch (8-cm) piece fresh ginger, grated

1 teaspoon salt

1½ teaspoons turmeric

Handful fresh coriander stalks, finely chopped

3 fresh green chiles, finely chopped

1 teaspoon chili powder

1 teaspoon ground cumin seeds

1 cup hot water

2 teaspoons Garam Masala (page 23)

1. Preheat the slow cooker on high (or to the sauté setting, if you have it). Then add the oil and let it heat. Add the onions and cook for a few minutes until they start to brown. Make sure you brown the onions well so you get a deep, flavorsome base.

2. Add the garlic and continue to cook on high for about 10 minutes.

3. Add the tomatoes, ginger, salt, turmeric, coriander stalks, chopped chiles, chili powder, cumin seeds, and water.

4. Cover the slow cooker and cook on low for 6 hours.

5. Remove the lid and stir. Let the masala cook for another 30 minutes uncovered to reduce a little.

6. Add the garam masala after the masala has cooked.

7. Use right away, or freeze it in small tubs or freezer bags. Just defrost what you need, when you need it.

PORTION TIP: This quantity will produce enough masala for at least 8 portions. I think it's really helpful to keep a base onion masala in your freezer for when you get that curry urge. Defrost what you need overnight, then put the masala in the slow cooker, add in your meat or vegetables, power on, and leave alone for 4 to 6 hours.

Homemade Greek-Style Yogurt

Dhai

⚙ QUICK PREP 🌿 VEGETARIAN | MAKES ABOUT 4 QUARTS

PREP TIME: 5 MINUTES | COOK TIME: 10 TO 12 HOURS (2 TO 3 HOURS ON LOW, PLUS 2 TO 3 HOURS TO COOL, AND OVERNIGHT)

Making yogurt always brings a smile to my face. I have such vivid memories of making dhai at home. In North India, yogurt is an important staple used for every meal. My mum had a designated brown ceramic pot and lid that was dedicated for making yogurt every few days. To start the process, she would send us over to the neighbors to get a pot of yogurt culture (whenever she ran out of her own). Quite often we forgot what we were sent for in the first place, and ended up playing with the kids, only to be shouted at when we hadn't returned an entire hour later. For a fresh and delicious dessert, add fruit (or fruit compote) to your homemade yogurt.

19 cups (4¾ quarts/
4½ liters) whole milk

1 cup plain yogurt,
at room temperature
(either from previous
batch or store-bought)

1. Pour the milk into the slow cooker set to low. Cover and cook for 2 to 3 hours. The temperature of the milk needs to reach 175ºF to 185ºF (80ºC to 85ºC). When it does, turn off the slow cooker, leave the lid on, and let the milk cool to 115ºF (46ºC). This will take another 2 to 3 hours.

2. When the temperature is right, in a small bowl add some of the warm milk to the plain yogurt. Stir to combine.

3. Stir this mixture back into the slow cooker, going up and down and side to side. Cover the cooker.

4. Wrap the slow cooker with a blanket or towel. Leave at room temperature overnight (10 to 12 hours). In the morning, the milk will have thickened and set.

5. To get a thicker consistency, strain the yogurt by lining a colander with some muslin or cheesecloth. Set it over a glass bowl. For a thick Greek yogurt, you will need to leave it to strain for about 3 to 4 hours.

6. When strained, refrigerate it in a glass jar for up to 2 weeks.

TECHNIQUE TIP: The yogurt you use as a starter must have live cultures inside, such as Lactobacillus bulgaricus and Streptococcus thermophilus. Invest in a digital thermometer to take the guess-work out of making dhai. Many new slow cookers have a yogurt setting, so do check for this, as such a feature can make yogurt preparation much easier.

Paneer

 VEGETARIAN | **MAKES 1 CUP**

PREP TIME: 10 MINUTES, PLUS SEVERAL HOURS TO STRAIN | **COOK TIME: 20 TO 25 MINUTES**

Paneer is an iconic North Indian ingredient that is used in many dishes. It's an amazing source of protein, especially beneficial for India's huge vegetarian population. This versatile ingredient can be used in chunks, grated into patties, or crumbled into vegetable dishes. It has the texture of tofu, and although creamy, its flavor is quite neutral. For your vegetarian friends, it's an amazing substitute for the chicken in the Old Delhi Butter Chicken (page 110). You can also use paneer to add protein to many of the vegetarian recipes in this book. Just treat it as you would any vegetable.

5¼ cups (1⅓ quarts/ 1¼ liters) whole milk

2 to 3 tablespoons lemon juice or white vinegar

1. Pour the milk into a large nonstick pan and heat on the stovetop over medium heat.

2. Just before the milk comes to a boil, right as it starts to bubble around the edges, add the lemon juice or vinegar, and stir. Remove from the heat and continue stirring. Let stand for 5 minutes.

3. The milk will separate into solid curd and whey (a watery liquid). If it hasn't separated, you may need to stir in a little more lemon juice or vinegar.

4. Line a colander with muslin or cheesecloth. Scoop the curd into the lined colander and let it cool. When cool enough to handle, pull the cloth into a ball and squeeze out any excess liquid.

5. If you want to use the paneer to crumble into a sauce, then just leave it in the cloth to hang over the sink (you can tie it to your faucet's bend) for 2 or 3 hours.

6. If you want a firmer, formed paneer (so you can cut it into chunks), then you need to weigh down the paneer to push out all the excess liquid. I usually put the cheesecloth bundle with the paneer in it over an upturned plate. Then I put another plate on top and weigh it down with my mortar and pestle, or with a pot filled with water. Liquid will ooze out, so set this in a deep pan or in the sink. Ideally, leave it to strain for at least an hour, but the longer you leave it, the firmer your paneer will be.

7. Finished paneer can then be cut into cubes and used as it is, or fried. Paneer also freezes really well, but do thaw it before cooking.

EASY ADJUSTMENT: You can flavor your paneer with toasted cumin seeds, chili flakes, black pepper, or fresh coriander leaves. Add these ingredients to the milk as you're heating it.

Plain Basmati Rice

⚙ QUICK PREP Ⓥ VEGAN | SERVES 6 TO 8

PREP TIME: 10 MINUTES | COOK TIME: 2 TO 3 HOURS ON HIGH

One of the most frequently asked questions I get is what the best way is to cook basmati rice. Indeed, there are many different ways to make excellent rice, but the easiest way is in a slow cooker—of course! Follow these few simple steps for fluffy basmati rice with perfectly separated grains, every time.

2 cups basmati rice

1 tablespoon butter or ghee

4 cups (1 liter) hot water
Pinch salt

1. Wash the rice in a few changes of water until it runs clear, and then soak it in warm water for 10 minutes.

2. Rub butter or ghee on the inside of your slow cooker.

3. Turn the slow cooker to high. Drain the rice and place it in the slow cooker. Add the water and salt.

4. Cover and cook on high for 2 to 3 hours. Check for doneness every 45 minutes. (This recipe typically cooks for me in about 2 hours and 15 minutes.)

- -

PORTION TIP: For a 2-quart (2-liter) slow cooker, halve the quantities. For a 6-quart model, add half again.

Whole-Wheat Flatbread

Roti or Chapati

VEGETARIAN | MAKES 10 TO 15
PREP TIME: 10 MINUTES, PLUS 30 MINUTES RESTING TIME | COOK TIME: 1 TO 2 MINUTES EACH

These flatbreads are an absolute staple of North Indian cuisine. I love roti and have been known to eat a fair few of them in one sitting. These are made from atta, which is a whole-wheat flour from crops grown across the Indian sub-continent. This is a hard flour, and it's made by grinding the whole of the wheat grain, which results in a light creamy-brown flour. Because atta has a high gluten content, the dough balls can be rolled out nice and thin and are easily toasted on a griddle pan until they puff up like little pillows filled with hot air. Making roti requires expertise, and it's a skill that Indian women are judged on. I have been making these since I was about nine, and even now my mother complains that they are not thin and round enough!

1 pound (500 g) atta, or half whole-wheat and half white flour	Water 1 teaspoon butter

1. Put the flour in a large bowl and, adding a little water at a time, rub to make crumbs. Continue adding a little water at a time to bring the flour together with your hands to make a soft dough.

2. Start to knead the dough right in the bowl, using your knuckles, folding it over as you go. The dough should come together and come away from your hands and the bowl. If it is sticky, add a little more flour and continue to knead. The dough needs to be soft but not sloppy. Cover and set aside at room temperature for at least half an hour before making the roti. This just gives the dough time to rest, not to rise.

Continued

3. When you are ready to cook the roti, heat the tava (an Indian griddle pan) or a heavy frying pan (cast iron is a great choice) on the lowest heat on the stovetop, and give it time to heat up evenly.

4. Put some dry flour on a flat plate for dusting. Flour your hands and take a tangerine-size ball of dough. Roll the dough in the palms of your hands to create a smooth ball. Flatten it using your fingers. Then holding the dough in one hand, rotate it around and flatten it out with the other hand.

5. Flour your hands again and begin to roll out the dough on a lightly floured work surface. Turn it over, dust the dough with flour, and roll again. Try not to let it stick to your worktop. If it does, just dust the surface lightly with flour.

6. When the dough is about 2¾ inches (7 cm) in diameter, pick it up and pass from one hand to the other as if you are clapping. This evens it out and removes the excess flour.

7. You need to form and cook the roti one at a time, so cook this one before you move on to the next one. Carefully place the roti flat onto the preheated pan. Try not to let the roti fold or wrinkle anywhere.

8. You will see the color of the roti darken after about 10 seconds; turn it over. If you're cooking on a gas stove, turn the heat down a little. When bubbles appear on top (after about 10 seconds) take the pan off the heat and put the roti directly onto the flame, using tongs. The roti will begin to puff up. Turn it over using tongs and move it around so it doesn't burn. Work quickly (this all happens in a matter of seconds), turning and pressing until it has all blown up. Be careful not to burn yourself. Remove the roti and set it on a clean kitchen towel and cover to keep warm.

9. If you are not using a gas stove or are not comfortable using a naked flame, leave the roti on the pan. Turn the heat down a little and when bubbles appear, turn the roti over. Using a clean kitchen towel, gently press the top of the roti and it will begin to blow up with hot steam. Remove the roti and set it on a clean kitchen towel and cover to keep warm.

10. Repeat until you have used up all the dough. Smearing the roti with a little butter on one side will keep them soft until you are ready to eat them with your meal.

INGREDIENT TIP: What's the difference between a roti and a chapati? Nothing, really. Roti are also known as chapati (or phulka), depending on which region of India you are from.

Naan

 **VEGETARIAN | MAKES 4**

PREP TIME: 30 MINUTES, PLUS 60 MINUTES RISING TIME | COOK TIME: 2 TO 3 MINUTES EACH

Wheat is a staple from North India and is used in many different ways across the country. From roti and kulcha (stuffed naan), to paratha (stuffed roti), North Indian dishes need some form of bread to finish off those deeply rich curries. Traditionally, naan is baked in a tandoor oven. The shaped dough is slapped on the inside wall of the tandoor, where it puffs up, leaving a bubbly, crisp top and a flat, seared bottom. Back in the day, many Punjabi villages would have a communal tandoor oven that could be used to cook naan, which was then shared with the community. Many restaurants today have tandoors in their kitchens, but this cooking method is difficult to mimic at home. This is my tried-and-true recipe, and it works beautifully.

1 teaspoon active dry yeast

1 teaspoon sugar

1 tablespoon warm water

1 cup white flour

1 teaspoon black onion seeds (or handful fresh coriander leaves, chopped)

½ teaspoon salt

½ teaspoon baking powder

1 tablespoon vegetable oil

2 tablespoons plain yogurt

2 tablespoons milk

1. In a small bowl, mix the yeast, sugar, and water to activate. Leave for 5 minutes in a warm place until frothy.

2. Meanwhile, in a large bowl, mix the flour, onion seeds, salt, and baking powder. When the yeast is frothy, add it to the flour, and then add the oil and yogurt.

3. Knead the dough with slightly wet hands, folding as you go. If it feels a little dry, add some milk and continue to knead. When it's nice and soft (about 4 to 5 minutes), return the dough to the bowl, cover the bowl with plastic wrap, and leave it in a warm place to rise for at least 1 hour (but longer if possible). The dough should be light and airy and should have doubled in size.

4. Turn on the broiler to heat up.

5. Punch the dough down. Then divide the dough into four balls and place one on a floured surface. Roll that ball out into a circle that's about ¼ inch (5 mm) thick.

6. Heat a tava or a large, heavy griddle (cast iron would be great) on the stovetop over high heat. Place the naan on the pan for a couple of seconds to brown on one side.

7. Transfer to a baking tray (seared-side down) and place under the hot broiler for 2 to 5 minutes, and watch the magic as it puffs up. Make one naan at a time. You can keep them warm by wrapping them in a clean kitchen towel until you are ready to serve.

8. Repeat with the remaining dough balls, until you have used up all the dough. Serve immediately (maybe smeared with a little butter!).

- -

SIMPLE SUBSTITUTION: No yeast in the refrigerator? You can replace it with 2 well-beaten eggs for a nice light naan.

Glossary

Chaat Tangy, sweet, spicy, and hot Indian salads that are very popular street food and snack dishes. The word chaat means "to lick," suggesting these dishes have a lip-smacking unique balance of flavors known as "chaat patta." Texture and color is just as important with these dishes, so they are served with two or three different chutneys (imlee, which is brown; mint, which is green; and a sweetened yoghurt). And they usually contain fried elements to give them a crunchy texture (either fried rice or seve, which are gram-flour crisps), soft spiced potatoes, and sometimes crisp fruit (like pomegranate seeds). These cold, refreshing salads are excellent choices for hot weather.

Curry Definitely not a single spice, curry is often sold as a blend of spices that are labeled "curry powder." Most curry powders include curry leaf, coriander, turmeric, cumin, fenugreek, and chile peppers. Unfortunately, curry has become a generic term to describe any Asian-style sauce dish with spices. The term is very wide and all-encompassing, and many cooks find it a little offensive, because it's rather extreme to group all saucy spicy dishes—whatever their origin (Indian, Thai, Chinese)—under a single name. But that is the way of the world, so we can't be too picky about it. I use the term "curry" for Indian dishes with a gravy.

Dhai A thick Greek-style yogurt.

Dhal This is a generic term Indians give to dried, whole, and split pulses, beans, legumes, and peas. The same word is used whether they are raw or cooked. Beans are usually larger than lentils, and for this reason generally require more cooking. These include red kidney beans, mung beans, and broad beans. Peas include dried peas, split peas, and chickpeas.

Gosht Tender, usually slow-cooked mutton or goat. Lamb is also referred to as gosht at most restaurants.

Kachumber A delicate salad made by chopping the ingredients into small-dice pieces. It's usually prepared with cucumber, red onion, chile, coriander, and tomatoes.

Korma Hailing from Mughal cuisine, korma is a dish where the meat or vegetables are seared on a high heat, then braised on a low heat for a long time at a temperature below the curdling point, slow cooking with water, yogurt, or cream. This dish had the prestige associated with the royal courts, using expensive ingredients such as saffron, cream, and poppy seeds.

Makhani or makhan The literal translation is "butter," but the butter in India isn't the same as the yellow butter we are used to in the West. Makhani is white butter that has a creamy texture and a pretty neutral taste. It can be made with cream or yogurt. Most Indian homes still make their own makhani every two or three days by churning fresh full-fat milk.

Masala Directly translated, it means "spice," but the term is also used to describe the base of curries and sauces made with onions, ginger, garlic, chiles, and tomatoes.

Murgh Chicken.

Naan A light-and-soft Indian flatbread made with leavened dough. It's traditionally cooked in a tandoor oven, where it's slapped onto the inside wall until it turns crisp and light.

Pandi Pork.

Paratha A flaky, fried Indian bread, usually eaten for breakfast. It's stuffed with spiced vegetables or eaten plain with pickles and yogurt.

Raita A yogurt-based side dish that has been embellished with spices, vegetables, and sometimes fruit. Yogurt provides the cooling element to a typical Indian meal, and so is served with all dishes. Raita can also be served as a dip for snacks.

Roti or chapatti A North Indian staple: unleavened flatbread made with atta, a hard-wheat whole-grain flour.

Sabji or sabzi The generic Hindi word for vegetables.

Shorba Spiced Indian soups are common in the cold winter months. The shorba wala (soup man) comes around with his cart of radiating soup which, when eaten, warms you from the inside out and effectively wards off any signs of a cold. They are usually a thin consommé style, rather than a thick Western-style soup.

Tarka Tempering spices or ingredients by heating them in oil and roasting them just enough so they crack open and release their fragrance into the oil.

Tava A round cast-iron Indian griddle pan that is smooth and concave in shape. It's used daily in the Indian kitchen to cook rotis and parathas.

Thoran The generic South Indian term for a dry (sauce-less) vegetable dish. Usually made with vegetables such as cabbage and jackfruit, and strong spices such as mustard seeds, black pepper, and curry leaves.

Resources

You'd be surprised what's available in supermarkets these days. You may not have looked closely at what's in the spice sections, or on the aisles labeled Asian, ethnic, or international. Because of their amazing medicinal properties, Indian spices (along with other exotic ingredients) also tend to be available at health-food stores.

And of course, you can get almost anything online. Here are some excellent online sources, depending on where you live. Other than fresh produce and meat, you can get anything mentioned in this book at these online vendors.

United States

www.indianfoodsco.com
www.ishopindian.com
www.kalustyans.com
www.patelbrothersusa.com
www.savoryspiceshop.com
www.myspicesage.com
www.penzeys.com
www.amazon.com

Canada

www.thespicetrader.ca
www.peppertreespice.com

United Kingdom

www.indianmart.co.uk
www.redrickshaw.com
www.spicesofindia.co.uk
www.theasiancookshop.co.uk
www.spicekitchenuk.com
www.natco-online.com
www.somayaskitchen.co.uk
www.harighotra.co.uk
www.amazon.co.uk

Australia

www.hindustan.com.au
www.indiabazaar.com.au

Conversion Charts

VOLUME EQUIVALENTS (LIQUID)

U.S. STANDARD	U.S. STANDARD (OUNCES)	METRIC (APPROXIMATE)
2 tablespoons	1 fl. oz.	30 mL
¼ cup	2 fl. oz.	60 mL
½ cup	4 fl. oz.	120 mL
1 cup	8 fl. oz.	240 mL
1½ cups	12 fl. oz.	355 mL
2 cups or 1 pint	16 fl. oz.	475 mL
4 cups or 1 quart	32 fl. oz.	1 L
1 gallon	128 fl. oz.	4 L

VOLUME EQUIVALENTS (DRY)

U.S. STANDARD	METRIC (APPROXIMATE)
⅛ teaspoon	0.5 mL
¼ teaspoon	1 mL
½ teaspoon	2 mL
¾ teaspoon	4 mL
1 teaspoon	5 mL
1 tablespoon	15 mL
¼ cup	59 mL
⅓ cup	79 mL
½ cup	118 mL
⅔ cup	156 mL
¾ cup	177 mL
1 cup	235 mL
2 cups or 1 pint	475 mL
3 cups	700 mL
4 cups or 1 quart	1 L

OVEN TEMPERATURES

FAHRENHEIT (F)	CELSIUS (C) (APPROXIMATE)
250°F	120°C
300°F	150°C
325°F	165°C
350°F	180°C
375°F	190°C
400°F	200°C
425°F	220°C
450°F	230°C

WEIGHT EQUIVALENTS

U.S. STANDARD	METRIC (APPROXIMATE)
½ ounce	15 g
1 ounce	30 g
2 ounces	60 g
4 ounces	115 g
8 ounces	225 g
12 ounces	340 g
16 ounces or 1 pound	455 g

Recipe Index

Index

Acknowledgements

They say it's not about where you end up, it's about the journey that gets you there—and I couldn't agree more! My journey up until this point has been pretty amazing. I have found new friends, new inspirations, new confidence, new skills, and so much more along the way, and it's all down to the amazing people I have met. The belief they have had in me has allowed me to grow as a cook and a person and, amazingly, it has led me to write this little book of recipes just for you.

My husband, Jeremy, who pushed me to start my cooking business one Christmas when he presented me with a laptop, some business cards, and a logo, and said "Off you go, do what you really want to do," has been by my side and is my chief recipe taster and critic. Without his support, I couldn't do any of it, so I thank you! Neyha and Jai for being prepared to taste everything that comes their way, even if it's not always with a smile! The Ghotras and the Kamaluddins, who are all awesome in their own way.

All my girlfriends (Lisa, Christine, Nicky, Nic) have supported all my events, doing everything from washing up to serving at my pop ups, and testing my curry kits and recipes. A huge thanks to all the guys at Jellyfish Ltd.—especially Rob Pierre, CEO, for being our friend and for believing that Hari Ghotra could be something special.

I am so very proud that Chef Vivek Singh took the time to share his wonderful words and thoughts about food with me and write the foreword to this book. Chef Peter Joseph has been an inspiration, mentor, friend, and teacher who has taught me so much about the ethos required in a professional kitchen—thank you.

The team at Callisto Media, who have made the process of writing this book so very easy, fun, and interesting.

The list goes on and on, but really it's always been about my mum and dad—my life inspiration. Mum for sharing all she knows in the kitchen and dad for showing me that by working hard anything can be achieved—I love you both, and I wish dad was still around to make me his mega-fish finger sandwich!

There isn't much we need in life to be happy, and surrounding yourself with great people helps. For me, cooking and food is about family, friends, love, and life. Having a wonderfully supportive family and fun friends who are always happy to sit around my dining table to share stories, food, and drink, to have a giggle with (and sometimes even to moan to) is a special thing. I hope this book helps you to share the love and pride I feel when I present a meal to my family and friends that's good, wholesome, fun, and delicious!

About the Author

Hari Ghotra is the founder of the biggest Indian food digital platform in the UK, featuring hundreds of easy-to-follow recipes, videos, and informative blogs. As a chef trained at Michelin-starred Tamarind's of Mayfair, Hari's passion for simplifying Indian food without losing authenticity and the flavors that the cuisine is know for, makes her one of the most sought-after cooking teachers in the UK. Her brand also extends to meal kits and spice kits, providing home cooks with quick and easy ways to make delicious, healthy, and authentic Indian food from scratch. She has been featured in the *Huffington Post*, the *Guardian*, and the *Independent*, among many others. She lives in London.

CPSIA information can be obtained
at www.ICGtesting.com
Printed in the USA
BVOW10s0500300817

492913BV00002B/2/P